More Than A Market:

Making Sense of Health Care Systems

Lessons from Community Voices: HealthCare for the Underserved

A Report Covering 1998 – 2002

www.communityvoices.org

September 2002

W.K. Kellogg Foundation
One Michigan Avenue East
Battle Creek, MI 49017-4058

Library of Congress Control Number: 2002109300

ISBN: 0-9722780-0-1

Foreword

As the largest initiative to be undertaken in the W.K. Kellogg
Foundation's seven decades of programming, *Community Voices:
HealthCare for the Underserved* represents commitments on a number of important levels. Certainly, the six-year investment in 13
communities across the United States represents a commitment of
significant resources to improving health care access and quality
for the most vulnerable members of our society. In 1998, at a time
when the so-called "safety net" of health care providers was buffet-
ed by public policy and market dynamics, changing demographics,
and rising rates of uninsured, Community Voices signaled the
Kellogg Foundation's commitment to exploring and developing
workable solutions to society's most intractable challenges –
solutions that could improve conditions in one community and
hold potential for many others.

But Community Voices also affirms our dedication to some
precious principles – beliefs that run across and through all
Kellogg Foundation programming. First of all, Community Voices
illustrates the measure of our belief in *community-driven change.*
We choose to invest in communities, in people, in their neighborhoods and organizations and providers. We do so because more
than 70 years of programming has taught us that, if given the tools
and resources, people in communities are powerful generators of
change for the better. Secondly, Community Voices underscores
our belief in *partnerships* knit together by strands of collaboration.
Health care delivery and financing, like health itself, are complex
and many-layered. No one entity at the community level has sufficient resources or influence to remake complicated systems.
Health care providers, public health, consumers, government,
business, and advocacy groups all grasp a piece of the solution –
and possess funds and expertise capable of transforming ideas into
action. And finally, Community Voices illustrates the Foundation's
conviction that system change needs *groundwork and preparation.*
We understand that change occurs only when the timing is right.
Windows open, public will shifts, and the inconceivable of the
past is ushered into the present. But if change has a cycle all its
own, the learning that precedes it – risks undertaken, ideas

explored, models tried and tested – are crucial to capitalizing on the timing. Readiness, we believe, can be cultivated and seed the way for change to take root and flourish.

The work of Community Voices grantees deepens these principles and extends what we understand about the process of change. Community Voices program efforts spring from their communities of origin, but link to regional, state level, and national issues. As Community Voices grantees have explored a wide range of ways to expand coverage and access for underserved populations and broaden the definition of health, they have formed coalitions and working groups capable of raising issues and marshaling resources to effect possible solutions. The 13 Community Voices projects in California, Colorado, Florida, Maryland, Michigan, New Mexico, New York, North Carolina, Texas, West Virginia, and the District of Columbia have become learning laboratories – working both individually and as a network to build on and extend our common understanding about community investments that produce measurable results. Throughout this endeavor, the voices of people in underserved communities, of health care professionals and administrators, and of civic leaders have been drawn into a dialogue, speaking out to share what they know and joining the chorus of those calling for change.

In this process, grantee efforts to expand access to health coverage and care for underserved community people are being strengthened by partnerships with other philanthropic organizations. Community Voices is collaborating with many private foundations – among them the American Legacy Foundation, The California Endowment, California HealthCare Foundation, Caring for Colorado, The Colorado Trust, The Duke Endowment, The Enterprise Foundation, Robert Wood Johnson, and Rose Community Foundation – as well as attracting support from federal agencies through grants from the Centers for Disease Control and Prevention and the Health Resources and Services Administration. This synergy is expanding the utility, relevance, and impact of Community Voices work.

Community Voices: HealthCare for the Underserved is mining a rich vein of pragmatic passion that runs through many communities – the hard-nosed determination to work with the resources at hand, blended with a hopeful idealism that envisions creating something better. Since Community Voices is at its midpoint as an initiative, the chapters that follow detail lessons to date. The processes and products described in this volume are offered to draw readers into an ongoing conversation about health, health care systems, and the potential of communities. Community Voices grantees do not claim to have found a magic potion for improving health systems, addressing cost issues, and fostering the well-being of people. But they have made impressive headway down a path that continues to daunt decision makers in corporate board rooms, public institutions, and the halls of state and federal government. What Community Voices grantees have to say about the potential to reorient health systems and improve health care – and about better use of scarce resources to meet the needs of people – is something many decision makers need to hear and heed.

William C. Richardson, PhD
President and CEO
W.K. Kellogg Foundation

Introduction

In 1998, the W.K. Kellogg Foundation launched a six-year initiative that would draw rural and urban communities from the West Coast, the East, and many places in between into a closely-knit collaborative working to increase access to primary care for the uninsured and underserved, and to strengthen the health care safety net in the process. The overarching premise behind the initiative was that the health care system did not work for everyone, especially people on the margins and the safety net providers they turned to for care. Even its name, *Community Voices: HealthCare for the Underserved*, is an unabashed statement of the initiative's intent – to place the voices least often heard in health care discussions front and center.

Today, what we call "Community Voices" is referred to in some circles as "a movement," in recognition both of the synergy it has produced and the scope of its impact. By inverting the decision-making pyramid, Community Voices grantees are doing more than reorienting their own local health services delivery, practice, and financing arenas. They are creating and piloting models for use on a larger scale and providing a venue for learning *how* to remake systems.

As a major health initiative in a Foundation with generations of health programming to its credit, Community Voices has been the beneficiary of many noteworthy ancestors. Its roots extend from health programs in rural Michigan prompted by the deprivations of the Great Depression to the strategic, comprehensive, community-based initiatives of the last 15 years. While the reach and breadth of Kellogg Foundation health programs has evolved, all reflect a deep commitment to community and the conviction that lasting change begins with people. Community Voices is born of this rich history.

Yet Community Voices is also a product of its time. In the late 1990s, Foundation program leaders saw the signs of potentially devastating shifts in the health care infrastructure. Changes in the economics of health services delivery – in financing; in reimbursement; and in growing demands on the systems providing care to working poor, immigrants, single men, people of color, and other marginalized groups – foreshadowed bleak times for many providers of last resort. An attempt to legislate a national health policy was still a bitter memory for many decision makers and, in its aftermath, marketplace ideology held sway. But "the market" was battering public hospitals, public health, academic health centers, clinics, and other safety net providers and threatening the few remaining health care resources earmarked for the most vulnerable community members.

Health, in fact, was getting lost in the marketplace shuffle. Foundation program staff knew only too well that uninsured and underserved people in communities often subsisted on a patchwork of health services for even their most pressing needs. What most Americans consider essential to maintain health – eye glasses, dental care, prescription drugs to treat illness – were far beyond the basic services provided to low-income working people, homeless, and others in emergency rooms and clinics. Even access to a regular source of care – the same doctor or group of medical providers – was beyond reach of the people without means to purchase health coverage. Health improvement within existing systems was an impossible dream for people outside of "the market."

In the face of these cold realities, Community Voices was conceived to increase access to care for the underserved, and to increase the capacity of health care systems to improve the health of communities. At the heart of the Community Voices approach was a dual charge: to create models responsive to local interests, resources, and needs that also would have bearing on public and institutional policy issues. By design, each Community Voices project would be both a working program and a learning laboratory.

Local solutions with national relevance – a tall order, but a practical one, Foundation program leaders reasoned. By linking programs with practice and policy, grantees' efforts would be more sustainable and the changes they promoted more permanent. And by relating local health care models to state and national issues, public and institutional policymakers – those with the most control over cost, quality, and other health financing and regulatory decisions – would have the potential to learn from Community Voices too.

Thirteen communities in 10 states and the District of Columbia recognized the opportunity Community Voices represented and accepted the challenge. Today, these 13 learning laboratories encompass many dozens of organizations and health systems, hundreds of community participants, and thousands of people no longer outside of the market.

In communities across the country, Community Voices projects have explored ways to strengthen the safety net for the underserved and improve health services delivery. In Baltimore, Maryland, the Men's Health Center provides primary care – physicals for work, illness care, mental health, and other services – to underserved men in the community. Many uninsured Detroiters and Lansing, Michigan, residents now have health coverage and access to prescription drugs and dental care. Clinics in Alameda County, California, and public hospitals in Denver and El Paso have programs and payment streams in place to care for thousands of people formerly without access to coverage. Children from low-income families in North Carolina, seniors in some New York City neighborhoods, and many uninsured in New Mexico have access to top-notch dental care. And these represent only a sampling of the programs underway.

Although just past the halfway point in their collective journey, the story Community Voices has to tell is a compelling one. Undoubtedly, more lessons will come. But those netted in the past three years contain useful information for the philanthropic community, policymakers in institutions and government, and community leaders in search of models for change – especially now. As employers wrestle with double-digit inflation in health costs, growing numbers of job holders and newly unemployed join the ranks of the uninsured. As the once surging economy slowly moves out of recession, leaders from Community Voices have much to say about where and how to invest in health systems when resources are scarce.

In the following chapters, we offer background on the Community Voices initiative and participants' advice and analysis to stimulate a broader conversation. Chapter 1 is a description of the challenges and opportunities Community Voices participants faced at the outset of the initiative – a look at the economic and political contexts surrounding health system decision making. Chapter 2 details the conceptual framework of the Community Voices initiative, its essential elements and time frame, as well as a brief description of each of the 13 learning laboratories.

Chapters 3 through 7 look across Community Voices projects to examine specific topics and explore promising approaches.

Chapter 3 looks at models for expanding coverage and improving access to health care. Chapter 4 describes efforts among Community Voices to identify oral health as a key component of community well-being and find ways to increase access to dental care. Chapter 5 illustrates the power of community interests in solving service delivery puzzles – the attitudes and approaches that have sparked Community Voices products. Chapter 6 describes how outreach, facilitated enrollment in existing plans, and care management fuel the collection of outcomes information and data to support and sustain system change. Chapter 7 highlights the role of leadership, partnerships, and relationships in promoting system change. Chapter 8 examines overall lessons for institutional and public policymakers, funders, and community leaders. At the conclusion of these chapters is a Resource Guide to help readers connect with Community Voices programs and identify other sources of information related to health, health systems, and promoting change.

Rather than a compendium of Community Voices work, the following is intended as an entrée to the wealth of ideas, data, and experience that initiative partners add to each and every day. Although the work continues, we believe the insights and experiences shared in these pages will serve to underscore the value of creating integrated, comprehensive health systems centered around primary care and prevention; illustrate the value of strengthening the health care safety net; and highlight some promising strategies for doing both.

Henrie M. Treadwell, PhD
Program Director
W.K. Kellogg Foundation

Table of Contents

Chapter 1:
More Than a Market – Health Care Realities

Face to face, the woman sitting before you has to be taken seriously. A 50-year-old grandmother working a minimum-wage job, Diane* is usually confident and accustomed to pulling her own weight. But when she talks about her health, a weary look surfaces and her eyes grow moist. "I can't afford the health insurance," she acknowledges. Without health insurance, without a regular source of health care, the emergency room is her doctor and she holds off going as long as she can. "I try to hold it in so I don't worry my girls," she says. "But when I had to go to the hospital, they knew how serious it was." A Midwestern hospital pharmacist mirrors Diane's discouraged stare as she explains an all-too-familiar scenario: "If the average person with health insurance gets three prescriptions, the person without insurance makes the choice to get two or one. We try to advise them, if they can't get them all, which ones they need to take." In a community a thousand miles away, a doctor articulates the frustration inherent in scenes like these: "I'm tired of seeing people with strokes because their blood pressure wasn't treated on time."

[*not her real name]

In any story about health care, it is easy for the listener to nod and quietly think, "That's unfortunate, but it's just one situation, one set of circumstances." But health care today is replete with stories like these – scenes that relegate the health of an individual to the end of a long line of confusing rules, obligatory costs, and accepted practices that control access to services, treatment, and payment mechanisms. Thus, one story is not solely about the high cost of coverage and prescription drugs or inappropriate use of emergency rooms or hurdles faced by the uninsured. Each is a telling tale about the health care system as it stands today and the barriers that ultimately determine whether a person will live well, limp along until a crisis occurs, or not live at all.

Diane's story also could be told by the doctors and nurses who see her in the ER or the hospital administrators who track emergency room use and costs in her community. It could be told by Diane's employer who notes her absences when she's doing poorly or by her children and grandchildren who shake their heads and say, "Mama's getting old." Any one health care story is, after all, the story of productivity and disability, of costs and benefits, of plusses and minuses on the balance sheet and in everyday life. What ails Diane, to some extent, also ails her family, her workplace, her community, and the institutions and businesses around her.

Admittedly, Diane's situation is only one story. And if hers was an anomaly, it would be easy to dismiss. But she is one of millions of people for whom existing systems do not produce care or promote health – working people without health coverage, those with no regular provider of health care, people lacking transportation or who do not speak English or otherwise cannot make their way through the systems in place. Diane is one of many, and each holds a clue to what could and should be changed.

The *Community Voices: HealthCare for the Underserved* initiative began when difficulties like Diane's were becoming more numerous because of political, social, and economic changes occurring in the larger environment. Editorials being written in early 2002 are describing a "perfect storm" of forces fueling the current health care crisis. But in 1998, those elements were off the public's radar screen and quietly gaining strength. An underlying assumption behind Community Voices was that heeding stories like Diane's could highlight the background issues troubling health care and guide the development of new models to promote care, access, and quality for underserved populations.

To better understand the intent and methods of Community Voices, one must appreciate the economic, social, and public policy issues at play in health care in the late 1990s – elements both familiar and emergent. At the end of the 1990s, health care was a rocky landscape – a place with sharp edges and pitfalls for safety net providers and the people who turned to them for health care services.

A Rocky Landscape

The Health Care Marketplace
In recent decades, the notion of the health care marketplace gained ascendancy and acceptance as a description of the U.S. health care system. Unlike the provision of public safety or fire services in a community, health care is not something all people

expect to receive simply because they reside in the United States. And although federal funds contribute to existing health systems through Medicare, Medicaid, and payments to support graduate medical education, health care is not something people expect to be provided through taxation or mandated through city, county, state, or federal entities.

We live in a society with a health care marketplace – a collection of businesses and enterprises available for purchase and operating under particular rules of commerce. If a house on Oak Street catches fire, we expect the local fire department to respond to the alarm whether Oak Street is an enclave for the city's wealthy or part of a low-income neighborhood. But if Diane cannot afford her blood pressure medication, that is Diane's problem.

> *As a society, we accept that some people receive **more** health care services than others because they have better coverage.*

Certainly it is true that nonprofit hospital systems hold that designation and tax-free status because they provide public services – and tangible community benefits like access to emergency care. It is also the case that the federal government contributes to the education of medical doctors, and that states regulate the provision of health care services and license many health professions. But as a society, we accept that some people receive *more* health care services than others because they have better coverage, more resources, and/or more ready access to care. That is simply how things are. Health care must be paid for and some have better payment mechanisms than others.

"System" in Name Only

Another distinctive feature of health care in the United States is the traditional reference to it as a system. Most would agree that there is no real system of health care in the United States – no working mechanism for the provision and payment of health care services across the board. In the absence of a national system – and some would say in reaction to an attempt by the Clinton administration to introduce such a system in 1992 – health care in the U.S. remains a patchwork of services and payment streams that can vary by municipality, region, and state.

The word "system" also implies coordinated allocation of resources or at least an organized method for determining how resources are used. But the funding for health care in the United States skews the allocation of resources toward provision of emergency and specialized services over primary care. Rather than invest in integrated delivery systems designed to keep people healthy by preventing serious illness, our payment streams ensure that the most expensive care will be provided when people do fall gravely ill.

For that reason, a person with the flu but no health coverage may be more readily seen in an emergency room than a private medical office in some communities. Likewise, an uninsured man with a bad tooth will probably have it pulled in the ER weeks before he could get an appointment in a dentist's office. Routine care for illness, regular dental cleanings, prescription drugs, eye exams and glasses, counseling and medication to help deal with depression – these are the things that keep people healthy and productive. Yet none of these are part of basic health care for many. These are extras available in selected markets to those with the right currency.

Medical Economics — Dollars, Not Sense

Any explanation for the range of services, access to care, and health coverage in the United States is inextricably linked to payment. Although Medicare and Medicaid are essentially single-payer systems, U.S. health care coverage is driven by an employer-based model. Access to coverage depends on the group a person belongs to – generally by virtue of employment or through membership in an employer group (such as the Chamber of Commerce in a given city or town or a small business association). Some municipalities offer community-rated coverage that allows individuals not otherwise affiliated to purchase health insurance. But individuals who cannot affiliate with a group through employment or some other type of membership are essentially out of the marketplace. They may be working. They may hold membership in community organizations or otherwise count themselves as part of various groups. But without a way to become part of an insurance-purchasing group with affordable coverage options, they are out of luck.

Another dimension that drives cost and limits coverage is the size of one's group. Very large corporations purchase coverage at rates that benefit their members. Very small groups usually pay much higher rates because fewer members assume the costs of care by way of premiums. Big purchasing groups have more members and, as a result, more clout to negotiate affordable rates for better coverage than smaller groups. Health insurance is a business designed to pay dividends to its investors like other businesses. So rates are calculated to ensure the solvency of the business, to limit its liability, and broaden its base of support.

Location is a related determinant of health care and coverage in the U.S. To some extent, population density drives the availability of health professionals and options for services. In a market-driven system, *where* one lives has a great deal to do with the care and coverage available. And the same holds true for health care providers with regard to reimbursement. The location of a hospital or clinic determines its access to funding streams and relative demand for services. Hospitals and clinics located in low-income communities function as the safety net for local residents without coverage or ready access to primary care. Thus, patients often arrive at their doors sicker and more in need of services than their counterparts in more affluent areas, but far less able to pay for the services they need.

Well-documented disparities in health outcomes – between people of color *with* health coverage and others – suggest there are more complicated forces at work in current systems that create barriers to health. Access to health coverage alone is not enough to ensure that underserved people will be better served by current systems, it seems. Despite advances in technology, pharmacology, and related medical sciences, African Americans and Latinos continue to suffer from higher rates of preventable conditions (hypertension, diabetes, poor oral health) regardless of their education, economic status, or proximity to health care resources. The relative lack of diversity among health professionals may be another indicator of systemic inequities that contribute to poor health and, eventually, greater health care costs. Even as the demographics of the general population continue to change, the relative proportion of students of color entering medical, dental, nursing, and other health professions schools remains very small.

Delivering Care in Good Times and Bad
Health care is a $1.3 trillion industry that includes hospitals, nursing homes, insurers, pharmaceutical and medical equipment companies, and other enterprises. In 2001, it was estimated to make

up 13 percent of the economy. But only a fraction of industry resources make their way to the so-called "providers of last resort" – the public and not-for-profit hospitals, clinics, public health departments, and academic health centers that comprise the health care safety net for the uninsured and underinsured.

In 1996, federal legislation reduced that slice of the pie even further. Cutbacks in Medicare reimbursement rates threatened the survival of those institutions even as related public policies – especially welfare reform – potentially placed greater demands on them. With fewer and fewer poor people eligible for assistance as a result of welfare reform, and considerable variation among state programs, the public safety net became more tenuous. Federal legislation fundamentally changed access to services for immigrants and made those who remained eligible wary of seeking assistance from any government agency for fear of being labeled a public charge. In a great many states, as people were moved off "the welfare rolls," many eligible people lost Medicaid coverage as well, eliminating a crucial payment stream for hospitals and clinics as they continued to provide care.

Legislation eventually restored some of the Medicare cuts and clarified Medicaid eligibility for former welfare recipients. But the vulnerability of the health care safety net was by then all too apparent. Despite the continued growth of the economy in the late 1990s, the number of uninsured remained fairly steady – between 40 and 44 million. More people were working, but many of those did not receive health coverage. Corporations were recording record profits, in part, because they were limiting their health care spending – providing coverage to fewer employees and moving to cost management through the managed care model to hold expenses down. And although many states later confirmed that most of the people making the transition from welfare to work remained eligible for Medicaid, those who had "fallen off" the rolls had left their mark on safety net institutions in the form of unreimbursed care.

So, as much money as there appears to be in health care, safety net providers know there is not much to be made in caring for the uninsured and underserved. From a medical economics perspective, the last few years of the twentieth century will be remembered

Only a fraction of industry resources make their way to the so-called "providers of last resort" – the health care safety net for the uninsured and underinsured.

as a time when health care spending remained flat. Managed care – held in contempt by many because of the constraints it places on health care spending – is largely credited with holding the line. But that was then.

Proponents and opponents of managed care alike generally agree that the short-term savings are over. And many on both sides recognize that the "savings" were created by cost shifting among varying levels of coverage – making it possible for the same care to cost more or less depending on whether a patient benefited from a managed care organization's negotiated rate or not. Since most safety net providers had no short-term savings anyway, they now find they have very little fat to pinch. Under the circumstances, the prospect of belt-tightening in the face of double-digit inflation in health care costs only becomes more problematic for these providers.

Issues on the Horizon

Economic and policy conditions are worrisome enough. But the solidity of safety net providers is also affected by societal changes and trends yet to emerge in full force. Shadow issues and demographics highlight gaps in current systems and point to far greater health care costs on the horizon.

Shadow Issues in Health Care

Any assessment of the cost of health care in the U.S. racks up impressive numbers. But issues seldom figured into the health care equation suggest that even greater expenditures are looming. Consider these statistics and their implications:

Almost half of adults in the United States do not have a single dentist visit in any given year. More than 108 million have no dental insurance. With the exception of emergency services, few oral health services are available for low-income adults and children without health coverage – those least likely to be able to afford to pay for dental care. Surgeon General David Satcher calls this a "silent epidemic" of dental and oral diseases that limits productivity and diminishes quality of life.

Each year an *estimated 28 percent* of adults in this country suffer from a mental health or substance abuse disorder, but only a fraction of those receive treatment. The direct and indirect costs of untreated mental illness – in terms of services, care, and lost productivity – fall on employers and educators, taxpayers and families. Yet misperceptions about mental illness remain widespread and the allocation of resources for research and treatment reflect the stigma attached to it. As Senator Pete Domenici of New Mexico noted at a press conference around mental health issues in his home state, "If, from the very beginning, all group health insurance had been compelled to cover mental illness like a heart condition, I believe we wouldn't be here today… There are more mentally ill in county and city jails than in all the hospitals treating mental illnesses." And, oddly enough, prisoners often receive treatment and medication in jail that they cannot access or afford when released.

Of the 11.6 million women between the ages of 55 and 64, more than *one in four* is divorced or widowed – making them three times less likely than their married counterparts to have an adequate income or health insurance coverage. The statistics for women of color point to even greater disparities. As individuals in this population group age, their health care needs rise even as their options for adequate income and health care benefits shrink. And the aging baby boomer generation promises to place greater numbers of people in this category – ensuring that the population of single women with very limited health care resources will grow in the decade ahead.

The staggeringly large U.S. prison population – more than 1.2 million men and women in state prisons alone – masks another potential drain on health care resources. As ex-offenders return to communities, their ability to gain employment is hampered not only by a prison record, but often by troubling health conditions as well. Ex-offenders are disproportionately men of color, who are more likely to face arrest and incarceration than their white counterparts. Men who have been in the criminal justice system generally reenter their communities with few prospects and no access to health care. Yet they may bring with them serious health problems, including substance abuse and mental health disorders, exposure to sexually-transmitted diseases, high blood pressure, diabetes, and other chronic health conditions. Without access to primary care and coverage, these men have no choice but to seek care through emergency rooms and free clinics. And by the time they seek care, the overall health of these citizens has been severely compromised – further diminishing their ability to seek job training and employment, or contribute to the well-being of their families and communities.

As pressing as these conditions are to the individuals who live with them – to older women, poor men, men and women newly released from prison, those struggling with mental illness, low-income people without access to dental care and coverage – the urgency from a societal perspective changes with the times. For instance, many states are accelerating the release of non-violent offenders in response to recent budget shortfalls. This trend will only add to the pressure on community hospitals and health departments to provide more services even as their budgets are reduced. Health care in the U.S. is a tangle of connections like these – "pushes" in one sector that create "pulls" in another.

> *"There are more mentally ill in county and city jails than in all the hospitals treating mental illnesses."*
>
> —Senator Pete Domenici, New Mexico

Demographics – More People Left Out of the Market
Another piece of the predicament for safety net providers is fewer insured working people and growing numbers of people with the least opportunity to access health coverage. Service industries, small businesses, and self-employed individuals represent a portion of the economy that has been steadily growing for a decade. As more people join the ranks of self-employed or work for businesses with fewer than 10 employees, the number of uninsured American workers climbs right alongside it.

Many self-employed or small business workers are young, educated entrepreneurs pursuing their dreams in a fast-changing marketplace. But many more are low-wage employees – former welfare recipients starting at the very bottom of the economic ladder; immigrant workers carving out places for themselves and their families. The people who work at the jobs no one else wants – in poultry processing plants, on hotel housekeeping staffs, in the kitchens of fine restaurants and fast food joints – are the least likely to have health coverage.

The shortcomings of the employment-based coverage model are glaring in the face of these trends. Census Bureau statistics indicate that even during recent economic boom times, the number of uninsured workers increased. Among full-time workers, 400,000 more people were uninsured in 2000 than in 1999. In businesses with fewer than 25 employees, only 31 percent had employer-based health coverage. Almost three-quarters of the uninsured in the U.S. live in a household with at least one full-time worker.

People of color and recent immigrants make up a disproportionate share of the low-wage workers who lack access to health coverage. Yet they also represent the fastest growing segments of the population nationwide. An estimated 800,000 people came to the United States in 1997 – half of those to join a family member, usually a working man already settled in the U.S. According to the Census Bureau in 2000, approximately 31 million people – or 11 percent of the population – were born outside of the United States.

In big cities, these may be the people driving cabs, serving meals, doing nails, and running mom-and-pop markets and dry cleaners. In rural areas, they are often the people moving from place to place picking fruit and harvesting crops. Whether born in this country or newly arrived, low-wage workers and small family businesses are the backbone of many community economies. Yet these are the people most likely to find themselves out of the health care marketplace – earning too much to qualify for federal programs, but too little to afford health care coverage and care.

Some Blue Sky

Community Voices safety net providers and community leaders – more mindful than the general public of the limitations of available resources and constraints on current systems – also recognized opportunities emerging from the health care system's rocky land-scape and the issues on the horizon.

Public Beginning to Search for Solutions
Although an attempt to legislate sweeping change in the nation's health coverage system stumbled early in the 1990s, by the end of the decade, many incremental changes were in process and health care was resurfacing as a troubling issue for many. A 1999 survey conducted for the Community Voices initiative by Belden Russonello & Stewart, a Washington, D.C., research firm, found strong support for changes in health care systems. Seventy-nine percent of those polled believed health care should be a right – something guaranteed to all – at the same time they voiced strong disapproval for the business of health care. While 75 percent of poll respondents advocated customizing health services to meet community needs, 85 percent claimed that much of the expense was created by the insurance industry. Health insurance bureaucra-cies, managed care practices, and the overall cost of health care were most often identified as problems in current systems.

Public frustration with attempts to manage health care costs by managing treatment decisions brought system issues to the fore throughout the decade. The public's perception of the insurance industry as one of many entrenched interests in the current system periodically pressured lawmakers into piecemeal legislative solu-tions. And although the 1990s did not produce the sustained pub-lic will to force a solution, growing dissatisfaction with systems and awareness of shortcomings represented an opportunity for engendering community solutions. Public health, provider, and academic and community leaders recognize that short-term cost issues are only the visible tip of the iceberg. The longer substantive change in existing coverage and care systems is delayed, the more serious the health consequences for uninsured and underserved people – and the greater the cost to provide care for them. People whose high blood pressure or diabetes goes untreated in their twenties or thirties or forties, for example, face far more debilitat-ing conditions in the future, and the cost of treatment grows accordingly. The costs of inaction to society in general may be deferred, but not delayed indefinitely.

11

Devolution of Policy Action to the State, Local Levels

Federal welfare reform legislation in 1996 provided another opportunity of sorts for sparking change in health care systems. The Personal Responsibility and Work Opportunity Reconciliation Act (PRWORA) shifted the power, authority, and responsibility for many safety net programs from the federal to state and tribal governments. This "devolution" of public policy to the state and local levels pressed these entities to assume a primary role in the genesis and enactment of policies and practices to move people from welfare to work. Such a dramatic shift changed the locus of control for programs and created greater expectations both of communities and the organizations and institutions serving them.

The crisis produced a pragmatic "we're all in this together" mentality that made collaboration appealing.

The pace and the scale of devolution resulted in confusion and tension among many welfare recipients and agency personnel, and increased pressures on safety net institutions. And the legislation that funded PRWORA, the Balanced Budget Act of 1997, made drastic cuts in Medicare payment rates to health care providers. Such sweeping across-the-board cuts threatened the viability of all safety net service providers – public and nonprofit hospitals, health centers and clinics, academic health centers, and public health departments. Yet the crisis produced a pragmatic "we're all in this together" mentality that made collaboration among institutions with differing interests not only possible, but appealing. For many, the incentives of collaborating outweighed the disincentives, and providers with disparate interests were willing to come together. By drawing on the collective local and state-level connections of a wide range of safety net providers, some leaders recognized the potential for pressing issues in a devolved policy environment.

Community Readiness – It's All in the Timing

At the community level, many safety net providers recognized another bit of blue sky. In response to past local health care crises – provider shortages in underserved areas, emergency rooms overwhelmed by demand for services, the threat of a for-profit hospital chain moving into an area – ad hoc groups of providers had come together in many communities. Some groups had disbanded as the crisis passed, but these forays into collaborative problem solving offered a potential building block.

Another opportunity took shape in the form of failed expectations of earlier efforts. For some communities, the investments of time and resources in past health initiatives contrasted badly with the return on investment. As one frustrated provider noted, "Millions of dollars have come through this community without having the impact it should have." Health indicators in some communities remain low, and racial and ethnic health disparities continue to grow. Lack of coordination of resources, turf issues, and "silos" of treatment and care in past efforts disappointed community members and providers alike. But those disappointments resulted in lessons that could be applied to new undertakings.

Most change agents agree that timing is everything.

Most change agents agree that timing is everything. For many Community Voices participants, the readiness of their communities – a combination of immediate need, community resolve, and lessons from the work that had come before – presented a rare opportunity. Without conventional wisdom to dictate a course of action, and with very little to lose given the political and economic climates surrounding them, these communities embraced Community Voices as a mechanism to address pressing issues and learn in the process.

Chapter 2:
Community Voices – Learning Laboratories Building Organized Systems of Care

- *"At the hospital they want the light bill, the water bill, pay stubs, papers for the house!"* exclaims a Florida farmworker to a translator. *"I say, 'I can't get all those things. I live at the county line – an hour and a half away!'"*

- *"I kept telling my coworkers, 'Don't call an ambulance! I can't afford it!' But they did anyway. That's another bill."* –Uninsured woman who suffered a stroke on the job.

- *"I had to take out a loan to pay for treatment,"* a doctor remembers. He had no choice. As a 23-year-old medical student already in debt for his education and just diagnosed with cancer, it was either take out the loan or postpone chemotherapy at his own medical center.

- *"How can the state fund stadiums and hotels when its citizens, who've paid taxes for years, are living in pain because they cannot afford medical care?"* –Question posed by a man attending a public forum.

Grantees were charged with shoring up local safety nets and developing models of care and coverage.

Blunt words and sharp rebukes for the health care system. But the most vulnerable – people without health coverage, without access to regular care, without the means to enter the health care marketplace – see its cracks at very close range.

Community Voices: HealthCare for the Underserved was conceived to draw on and learn from experiences like these. The initiative targeted building cost-effective, sustainable health care delivery systems to address the needs and interests of underserved in their communities. Using the resources available and finding new ones, Community Voices grantees were charged with shoring up local safety nets and developing models of care and coverage that might point the way for practices and policies nationwide.

After three years of work, Community Voices project leaders believe the approach already merits consideration by decision makers in other venues. The opportunity to build systems, as one Community Voices participant put it, "in real time, not on paper" has improved access to health services for many of the most vulnerable, and changed the way community hospitals, university health systems, public health departments, and community-based organizations are working together and independently.

When asked, Community Voices participants can readily identify the features of the initiative that have contributed to its progress – features that explain the concept, processes, and scope of the initiative in greater detail. In this chapter, these seven distinctive elements of the Community Voices approach are examined and the 13 projects, their partners, and targets, briefly described.

A Framework, the Resources, and Time

"Change doesn't happen in a year or two."

Community Voices: HealthCare for the Underserved promised funding and other resources to potential grantees. But Community Voices participants believe that the financial investment was only one of the inducements to participate and persevere. In comments throughout the initiative, they emphasize that the conceptual framework of the initiative and its time frame were equally appealing.

To guide partners and help them focus their energies, the Community Voices initiative developed a set of four broad outcomes and nine core elements. Taken together, the outcomes and elements create a framework for action in each of the projects. Embedded in these statements, grantees say, are important principles that attract a wide range of partners, and enough specifics to center the work and hold their collective feet to the fire.

The four outcomes – sustained increase in access for the vulnerable, a strengthened community safety net, cost-effective and high-quality delivery systems, and models of best practices – raised the bar for grantees. The outcomes make it clear that Community Voices is not only about services or reimbursement, but about the opportunity to create systems that make sense to the people who need them.

Nine core elements explain the Community Voices task more fully. Based on lessons from decades of W.K. Kellogg Foundation health programming, these elements impart a wealth of information to grantees about successful strategies for promoting change that other Foundation grantees have refined over time. Thus, Community Voices participants took up their work knowing they would need:

- A plan for informing public and marketplace policy;

- A strategic plan to develop and refine a cost-effective delivery system;

- Linkages to public health;

- Broad involvement of key community players;

- An infrastructure to hold the provider and community network together;

- Explicit response to the community's context for creating health and wellness;

- Effective use of resources to attain system change;

- Readiness of the lead participants and their leaders to spearhead the project; and

- Capacity to function and serve as a laboratory for system change.

Community Voices participants admit that, at the outset, the initiative's outcomes and elements represented a complicated set of objectives. Yet they report that, within the framework of these statements, each Community Voices project has enjoyed great latitude to devise and enact an approach to system change depending on the community's point of departure and state of readiness. In some communities, for example, convening groups and creating a forum for drawing community, providers, and advocates together has been a lengthy process. In others, the connections were in place and the crux of the work has been on marshaling resources to support a plan on the table. Community Voices targets and methods vary from project to project. Yet, they are eminently suitable to their communities and local issues.

Participants add that having enough time to tackle the tough issues is a big part of the equation, from their perspective. Many partners come to the table as competitors in the health care marketplace. Community Voices participants say the initiative's six-year time frame and commitment on the part of the Kellogg Foundation is giving them time to meet, to develop a common understanding, and to address conflicts and build trust. With time, Community Voices is making it possible to move beyond ad hoc committees and one-size-fits-all approaches to build lasting structures that support change.

Many Leaders, One Broad Network

"We are all significantly different and our diversity is a strength for the Community Voices collective effort."

In selecting the lead partner in each Community Voices project, the Kellogg Foundation illustrated just how broad health system change partnerships need to be. As project descriptions later in this chapter will demonstrate, Community Voices grantees are public health departments, academic health systems, public hospitals, and community-based or advocacy organizations. Rather than identify a single type of institution to take the lead, Community Voices intentionally reached out to a wide range of community health stakeholders. As such, the Foundation looked to the community to identify the organization or group willing to serve as a convener to draw the providers, institutions, consumers, and the community as a whole into the endeavor.

Community Voices intentionally reached out to a wide range of community health stakeholders.

By tapping a variety of lead organizations, the initiative has drawn many distinct organizations into one broad Community Voices network. Through regular networking meetings, conference calls, on-line connections, and informal one-on-one conversations, Community Voices participants learn firsthand the perspectives of institutions and organizations operating in and around health care systems. Across the initiative, academic health system administrators and public hospital administrators come together with community advocates, public health directors, and outreach workers. Together they explore and debate the relative merits of strategies and learn from one another. And in doing so, they mirror the polyglot collaborative workgroups forming in their own communities.

In the course of the initiative, approaches tried in one Community Voices project often are picked up by another as participants pool their growing understanding and share ideas. And Community Voices projects have formally collaborated in some beneficial ways too. Community Voices served as the model for the Community Access Program (CAP) – a $200 million Federal Health Resources and Services Administration (HRSA) effort to support programs for the uninsured and underserved.

Although operating in very different parts of the country under widely varying policy and practice conditions, Community Voices participants see themselves as part of a progressive movement to reorient health systems to better meet the needs of people. This is, in part, an outgrowth of the diversity among organizations taking the lead and a byproduct of the active collaboration across projects that is attracting and leveraging tangible support and creating a wider community of interests.

Clear Focus on People

"In every other business, you look to your customers to tell you what to do. But not in health care."

The Community Voices initiative has made its tag line "HealthCare for the Underserved" the fulcrum for grantee efforts – at times a guiding principle, a call to action, and a decision-making tool. Consistent with the general thrust of Kellogg Foundation health programming – and its programming overall – the design of the Community Voices initiative helped grantees place people – their well-being, their issues – in the foreground of project efforts. Rather than relegate the difficulties of those on the margins of traditional health care delivery systems to a minor role, Community Voices has given grantees a reason to take their experiences seriously and draw on their perspectives.

The design of the Community Voices initiative helped grantees place people in the foreground of project efforts.

19

The effect, Community Voices program leaders explain, has been galvanizing. By listening to and learning from the most vulnerable in their communities, Community Voices partners have been able to identify gaps in local systems and begin to correct them. Focusing on people also has given Community Voices partners a way to cut through traditional approaches and manage conflict. As one Community Voices program leader notes, "Our work is not about partners, but about people. If it benefits people, our duty is to go forth." By actively seeking to engage the hard to reach, Community Voices projects are finding more efficient ways to allocate resources and measure results.

Connecting Programs, Practice, and Policy

"Don't be discouraged if you can't make major changes overnight."

Community Voices required grantees to develop plans and strategies that would inform both best practices and policy options. Grantee program leaders and partners say this feature of the initiative has made them more aware of the practice and policy implications of their work – and more likely to disseminate information and share experiences with colleagues, related organizations, and public policymakers.

Kellogg Foundation program staff recognized that without this emphasis even the most laudable programs would have limited impact. Surely, the issues Community Voices grantees would confront in their local systems were at play in communities and systems across the country. Any solutions they developed and tested – to expand coverage to low-income workers, to provide access to care for underserved, to streamline systems for greater efficiency – could hold the key for other communities or inform policy options at the state or federal levels.

With that in mind, Community Voices places an emphasis on the practice and policy dimensions of local work and provides technical assistance, resources, and networking opportunities to increase the capacity of grantees to pursue their targets. A Community Voices Resource Team of communication, policy, and evaluation organizations help grantees gather information, refine messages, and choose targets. A common website (www.communityvoices.org) supports dissemination of information about local project efforts and connects site-specific work with wider communities of interest. Grantees believe these features of the initiative's design are making their work more strategic, more relevant to issues, and more lasting.

'Health' Writ Large

"Community Voices puts issues 'out there' – access, oral health, mental health."

Marketplace language speaks to specific services and treatment codes, narrowing the pursuit of health by defining smaller and smaller parts of a multi-layered whole. By contrast, the Kellogg Foundation's Health Programming Goal articulates a broad brush definition of health, emphasizing "increased access to integrated, comprehensive health care systems that are organized around public health, prevention, and primary health care." From this perspective, health encompasses many aspects of community life and links health improvement to economic conditions, workforce development, and the role of institutions in promoting community change.

Community Voices projects are challenged to see health as broadly as underserved groups view it – to recognize the relationship between economics, the availability of services like dental care or substance abuse treatment, and community well-being. In doing so, they wrestle with health in all its complexity. Access to care is a good example of this broad view. Some health delivery system administrators might define access to health care as whether or not a person in X community could see X provider. But Community Voices projects consider a range of issues with bearing on access to appropriate and timely health care – financial barriers (adequate coverage for services or for the purchase of medications), geographic barriers (distance, lack of transportation, travel time), and cultural barriers (language, understanding, acceptance of health care professionals or treatment).

By taking the broad, human view of health and health care – what a person needs to be well, what gets in the way of good health – Community Voices program leaders say their efforts are deepening community understanding about health issues and raising expectations of health systems. In this scenario, health-related institutions (public health departments, academic health systems, hospitals, and others) are in a unique position to act as sentinels and lightening rods – to stimulate collaboration, inform policy discussions, and promote community-oriented systems change.

Fostering Diversity, Community Participation

"Community Voices got us beyond 'guys in ties.' This approach is the opposite of getting a few key people in a room to put something on the fast track."

The Community Voices model requires grantees to reach beyond traditional health care decision-making circles in the development and enactment of solutions. Community Voices projects actively engage the people most affected by safety net systems – the uninsured, low-wage workers, people of color, immigrant families – not only to help define the scope of issues, but to add their insights to the redesign of systems. Community forums have evolved into workgroups and advisory bodies that bring health system and public health administrators together with the people their systems serve. In doing so, grantees say they have discovered capable allies whose interests and voices can drive system change.

Community Voices projects actively engage the people most affected by safety net systems.

Community Voices projects are tapping churches, neighborhood organizations, economic development coalitions, and other partners to link with and engage community members. By making community participation a central feature of the Community Voices model, many grantees acknowledge that their projects better reflect the diversity of their communities. In the process, Community Voices believes it is establishing broader, deeper roots in the community – connections with the potential to sustain program efforts long after the grant period concludes. Across the initiative, Community Voices also is demonstrating effective techniques for engaging community members that reflect the growing diversity of the United States – methods and experiences that can inform decisions made in other states and at the federal level.

Products that Make Process More Credible

*"Community Voices broadens the scope of solutions and strategies –
to think beyond the walls of the medical center and clinic."*

In addressing individual community needs and interests, each
Community Voices site has undertaken the development of specific products. Rather than requiring that each grantee pursue one
specific method or another, the openness of the Community
Voices model has made it possible for many types of products to
emerge – technological solutions to tracking enrollment or case
management in one venue; redesign of patient visits in another. As
a result, Community Voices projects have gathered and disseminated data; released reports; created and piloted technology to track
services; and developed new services, redesigned service delivery
methods, and established new service venues.

The tasks Community Voices undertakes seek to overcome
stumbling blocks – one piece of the larger puzzle of expanding
coverage or improving access. But grantees say these products also
have animated the process, attracted new partners and resources,
and moved them closer to long-term objectives. Products developed through the efforts of one Community Voices project are
shared with others in the network – often spurring replication or
collaboration across sites. Grantees believe that the synergy of
product development has served to energize the work, focusing
efforts within and across Community Voices partnerships.

Community Voices Projects

In 1998, the Kellogg Foundation initiated a competitive process,
selectively inviting proposals from qualified institutions and organizations based on their demonstrated capacity for innovation and
their readiness to undertake work on the scale of the Community
Voices framework. Thirteen grantees were chosen for the power
and potential of their proposed projects to serve as demonstrations
and laboratories for systems change. The Foundation's intent was
to test, document, and disseminate different approaches generated
by communities with varying circumstances, resources, and policy
contexts – communities that reflected the growing diversity of the

23

nation. Another intention was to explore solutions in both rural and urban communities, in densely populated and remote areas, and among very diverse and homogeneous populations. To better appreciate the scope of the initiative, consider the variety of lead partners, geographic locations, target populations, and project activities in each of the 13 Community Voices projects:

Alameda County/Oakland, California

Two established community health centers – *Asian Health Services* and *La Clinica de La Raza* – are taking the lead in Oakland Community Voices. Working in collaboration with the Alameda Health Consortium, the two lead partners administer the Oakland site project. Community Voices for Immigrant Health, as the Oakland project is known, is targeting uninsured immigrants in Alameda County. Of the 140,000 uninsured, 53 percent are immigrants. Traditionally, immigrants have faced economic and cultural barriers in accessing health care systems. Since welfare reform policy eliminated immigrants from the health care safety net in 1996, they have faced policy barriers as well. As the size and diversity of California's population continues to grow, California communities address, on a large scale, challenges and issues facing many communities.

To expand coverage and access for the uninsured in Alameda County – regardless of immigration status – Oakland Community Voices is building on strategic partnerships and longstanding relationships that reflect the lead partners' years of service. Working with its partners, including the Alameda Alliance for Health, a local nonprofit, managed care plan, Oakland Community Voices developed Alliance Family Care, a subsidized, affordable health care coverage product. In another major undertaking, Oakland Community Voices took the lead in collaboration with the University of California-Los Angeles Center for Health Policy Research to conduct, analyze, and disseminate the first multi-language, county-specific survey of its kind to focus on uninsured adults. Since its release, the County of Alameda Uninsured Survey (CAUS) is providing crucial baseline data to health systems, advocacy groups, and governmental entities. Oakland Community Voices also initiated the Access to Care Collaborative, a group dedicated to expanding coverage and access to care for the county's uninsured. The Collaborative is bringing together leadership across the county including the Alameda Alliance for Health, the Alameda County Health Care Services Agency, the Alameda County Medical Center, the Alameda County Social Services Agency, and the Alameda Health Consortium.

Albuquerque, New Mexico

The *University of New Mexico (UNM) Health Sciences Center* is the lead partner in Community Voices New Mexico. The UNM Health Sciences Center actively collaborates with the New Mexico Department of Health; the New Mexico Human Services Department; First Choice Community Health, Inc.; the Indian Health Service; and many public and private hospitals, managed care organizations, and community groups. Community Voices Shared Solutions, the New Mexico Voices project, targets New Mexico's underserved urban and rural residents. In doing so, the project addresses disparities driven by geographic size, location of services, and limited resources. The state has one of the highest rates of uninsured in the United States – 25 percent. The fifth largest state geographically, two-thirds of New Mexico's population lives in remote, rural areas. Yet most of the state's health care providers practice in urban centers.

To address these and other challenges, Community Voices Shared Solutions is building partnerships that draw provider, state policy, and advocacy groups into a "health commons" approach – an overall network of care designed to expand community-based, integrated primary care services for New Mexico's uninsured and underserved, and use scarce resources more efficiently. Beginning with two counties, Shared Solutions is learning ways to expand health coverage, coordinate and improve care, and lower costs. In Bernalillo County, more than 15,000 uninsured residents have been enrolled in the UNM Care Plan, a primary care network. Bernalillo County enrollees receive a UNM Care Plan card that ensures access to an apparently "seamless" system of care based on the plan's benefit package. But the primary care services reflect high levels of collaboration among the UNM University Hospital, the school of medicine, and community health centers. Shared

Solutions' Oral Health Initiatives reflect similar levels of collaboration. In a state with no dental school and one of the lowest dentist-to-population ratios in the U.S., Community Voices' focus on oral health has expanded coverage and access to dental services for the most vulnerable, established a UNM division of dental services, and sparked public health and interdisciplinary opportunities to include oral health concerns in primary care practices.

Baltimore, Maryland

Baltimore's *Vision for Health Consortium* joined core partners – The Enterprise Foundation, the Baltimore City Health Department, Bon Secours Baltimore Health System, Total Health Care, the University of Maryland Medical System and School of Nursing, and Community Building Partnership – in a community-driven health initiative. In July 2002, to promote sustainability, the Baltimore City Health Department became the grantee and the lead partner. Baltimore Community Voices serves Sandtown-Winchester, a 72-block community of 10,500 residents, most of whom are African American. The program is targeting improved coverage and access to health care in a community with high rates of unemployment, substance abuse, and uninsured or underinsured people. To improve overall community health and respond to pressing community issues, Baltimore Community Voices activities encompass violence prevention and addressing the needs of recently released ex-offenders as well as traditional health services delivery.

Baltimore Community Voices collaborated with the Baltimore Health Department to open a Men's Health Center, the nation's first full-time, full-service primary care facility for uninsured men and a model being replicated elsewhere. Working with the University of Maryland School of Dentistry, Baltimore Community Voices' school-based health center dental program provides oral health care, including dental sealants to prevent cavities, to elementary school children and provides instruction on brushing and flossing at home. Vision for Health works with grassroots organizations to raise issues related to community health. Women Against Violence creates a forum for local women, many of whom have lost a child to violence. The group works to mobilize residents to address the physical and mental health consequences of violence. Vision for Health also was instrumental in the formation of the Maryland Citizens' Health Initiative Education Fund (MCHIEF). MCHIEF launched "Health Care for All," a statewide citizens movement that represents 2,200 organizations across the state working to increase access to affordable health care coverage.

California Native Americans

The *California Rural Indian Health Board (CRIHB), Inc.* is the Community Voices grantee focused on increasing the availability of health care services to Native Americans in rural California. An organization founded in 1969, CRIHB joins 34 tribes and 10 tribal health programs in an effort to improve access to care in 17 predominantly rural counties. Representing a network of tribal health programs controlled and sanctioned by Indian people and their governments, CRIHB is dedicated to improving the health status of people – both tribal members and the non-Indians who actively use tribal health programs in their service areas. Indian people in California, as elsewhere, have significant health issues to address. Native American communities suffer very high rates of diabetes, hypertension, alcohol and drug addiction, and other chronic health problems. Yet their tribal health programs are chronically underfunded, creating strains on tribal health providers working within a weak infrastructure and on limited resources.

Through Community Voices, CRIHB is spearheading the development of an efficient system of care for Native Americans – a culturally-competent, statewide system that maintains the traditional Indian Health Service focus on public health, but functions as an Indian-owned, managed care organization. As part of this process, CRIHB has informed the development of an actuarial policy for allocation of resources through the Indian Health Service. At the center of CRIHB efforts is the creation of Turtle Health Plan, the first statewide, managed care organization created by and for American Indians. Twenty-one Indian health programs in 36 counties, representing 69 tribal governments, have committed to the Turtle Health Plan to date. A Turtle Health Plan board of directors has been established and entrusted with the responsibility for overseeing the development of this risk-holding entity.

Denver, Colorado

Denver Health, a public hospital system, is a primary safety net provider in the largest urban center in Colorado. Through an integrated health delivery system that includes Denver Health Medical Center, federally qualified health centers (FQHCs), school-based clinics, and public health, Denver Health is the primary care and inpatient hospital provider for one in five Denver residents – many of them uninsured or underinsured and low-income, including many Latinos, African Americans, Native Americans, and Asian Americans. As part of the Community Voices initiative, Denver Health identified three opportunities for expanding access to coverage and care for vulnerable populations and strengthening the safety net – inadequate outreach, lack of enrollment in existing public programs, and poor care management. By drawing on the infrastructure and contacts within Denver Health and actively partnering with the Colorado Department of Health Care Policy and Financing, the Colorado Child Health Plan, the city and county of Denver, Denver Public Schools, Colorado foundations, local and statewide coalitions, and others, Denver Health has pursued these targets and identified others for improving health and increasing health system effectiveness.

Denver Health Community Voices has initiated a community outreach program that employs community health advisors from Latino, African American, and Native American communities to connect with hard-to-reach populations. In partnership with the Community College of Denver, Denver Health Community Voices has developed a Certified Community Health Worker curriculum to expand the pipeline of capable outreach workers. In 2000, the Denver Health Facilitated Enrollment program enrolled 74,000 uninsured into coverage options they were eligible for, including Medicaid, the Child Health Plus program, and the Colorado Indigent Care Program. To support the enrollment process, Denver Health developed and piloted AppTrack, an application tracking database. Denver Health Community Voices has also undertaken a randomized, controlled study to demonstrate that case management of chronically ill adults improves health outcomes and lowers costs.

Detroit, Michigan

The *Voices of Detroit Initiative (VODI)* was formed as a collaborative partnership among Detroit safety net providers – the city of Detroit Health Department, Detroit Medical Center, Henry Ford Health System, and St. John Health System. In a metropolis where one-fourth of the population draws on safety net providers for health services and an estimated 247,000 people have either inadequate coverage or none at all, the issues facing providers are significant. Community health challenges – including high rates of hypertension, obesity, and other chronic health conditions – are equally daunting. Although Detroit mirrors the problems facing many large cities (poverty, disparities in income and health status, racism), it has a history of chronic underfunding for primary care given its population, and lacks a public hospital system to serve the most vulnerable. To address cost and care issues, VODI is pooling the resources and insights of founding partners as well as academic institutions, community health centers, and community-based service and advocacy organizations to improve care for the underserved and expand the capacity of the systems serving them.

VODI is drawing on these relationships to form an Integrated Service Delivery Network for the uninsured in Detroit. A first step has been establishing and piloting an organized system of care for a portion of the uninsured that enrolls uninsured, and manages and tracks care. Referred to as a "virtual managed care" system, Detroit adults who meet income guidelines and are not eligible for Medicaid or another program receive an identification card that links them to a provider network and tracks services through billing data. A related thrust of VODI's efforts has been to expand primary care access points to enroll eligible people in existing programs. VODI partners also are collaborating to expand primary care health system capacity for city residents. A Pharmacy Access Program, the creation of a full-service dental clinic for uninsured adults, increased funding for primary care in the city – these changes reflect the level of collaboration at work through VODI efforts and improved care options for Detroit's underserved.

El Paso, Texas

Community Voices El Paso is a partnership of 24 organizations and institutions – entities that include health and human service organizations, academic institutions, local coalitions, city and county governments, health professions organizations, community-based organizations, and advocacy groups. At the outset of Community Voices, Thomason Hospital, the public hospital in El Paso, took the lead in convening health providers from the public and private sectors in El Paso and Ciudad Juárez, Chihuahua, Mexico. Since that time, the providers and community groups working with the growing population along the U.S.-Mexico border have become active partners in Community Voices El Paso's efforts to address the health care and access issues facing the uninsured, the medically underserved, and the binational workers who routinely travel across the border. In doing so, partners address culture and language barriers, chronic disease issues, and provider shortages with a perpetual lack of resources. El Paso's rates of poverty and uninsured are some of the highest in the United States.

Community Voices El Paso initially worked to identify options for expanding coverage and care by gathering information, developing a managed care plan, and conducting focus groups to identify community perceptions of the most pressing health issues. The El Paso Primary Health Plan was opened to enrollment in spring 2001. Since that time, it has enrolled approximately 7,000 uninsured. Community-based organizations are conducting enrollment. La Linea de Salud, a 24-hour community call center staffed by nurses with follow-up conducted by *promotoras* (health workers from the community), has been established to handle health questions and serve as an access point for primary care. Community Voices El Paso also provides leadership to the West Texas Child Health Insurance Program (CHIP) Collaborative, a highly successful enrollment strategy that coordinated local organizations and community links to enroll eligible children in the Texas Child Health Insurance Program.

Lansing/Ingham County, Michigan

The *Ingham County Health Department* originally convened a core group of partners (Sparrow Health System, Ingham Regional

Medical Center, and the city of Lansing) to form Ingham Community Voices. But the number of partners swelled to 18 as the Ingham Community Voices process has unfolded. Neighborhood organizations, public school districts, the police department, and many rural and urban community-serving organizations are actively engaged in expanding coverage and care options for the uninsured in Ingham County and developing an organized system of care. With many working families struggling to access care, and between 30,000 and 34,000 uninsured people in the county, Ingham Community Voices developed a mechanism to draw health care providers, purchasers, insurance companies, and consumers into a dialogue about health care.

Over many months, Ingham Community Voices conducted interviews, solicited perspectives, and shared what they learned with ever larger groups of stakeholders – expanded over time to reach African American, Latino, and other local underserved populations. Dialogue led to recommendations, and recommendations to the development of an action plan for Ingham County. The working relationships and connections forged in that process are driving project activities now. The Ingham Health Plan, a benefit plan for low-income uninsured, has enrolled more than 14,000 people thanks to targeted marketing and grassroots outreach. The Ingham Health Plan Corporation that manages the plan has a representative board of directors that includes at least two plan enrollees. In related programming, the Capital Area Prescription Program provides discounted prescription drugs to participants from Ingham and two nearby counties. An oral health focus has led to the development of dental care services for more than 3,000 adults and children annually. And a patient visit redesign effort – another thought planted in discussions about health care delivery – is reorienting the patient visit process in two Ingham health centers.

Miami, Florida

Community Voices Miami is built on the commitment and knowledge of three experienced core partners – *Camillus House, Inc.*, a homeless shelter serving Miami-Dade's most vulnerable; *RAND*, a respected research organization; and *United Way of Miami-Dade*, a conduit to local community-based organizations addressing the needs of underserved people. In this culturally diverse metropolitan area of two million, Miami's uninsured and underserved – many of them immigrants, low-income workers, or homeless – represent a significant population. Community Voices Miami is working to build a collaborative health care environment that coordinates the allocation of health care resources to better meet the needs of underserved people. To that end, Community Voices Miami has initiated a thoughtful, systematic process to engage stakeholders, draw area safety net providers and community-based organizations into dialogue, and form relationships to support ongoing collaboration.

As part of this long-term strategy, Community Voices Miami has established a Multi-Agency Consortium to make recommendations and guide the development of an action plan for Miami-Dade County. United Way of Miami-Dade sponsored 21 community dialogues – sessions that prompted more than 600 community members to share their perspectives on access and care issues. Information about barriers that surfaced in these dialogues prompted the development of streamlined processes for uninsured seeking access to services and the elimination of some fees for underserved community members. Project efforts also have led to the development and release of reports on Miami-Dade health care financing and hospital care for the uninsured – to help business leaders and other stakeholders understand how funds flow through the system. A report on dental services available to uninsured in Miami highlighted area shortages and resulted in additional funding and new partnerships to address unmet needs. Community Voices Miami is pursuing these and other opportunities – including an innovative youth program – to build on a growing consensus about issues, resources, and ways of working together to better meet the needs of Miami-Dade's underserved residents.

North Carolina

FirstHealth Community Voices is based in Pinehurst at *FirstHealth of the Carolinas, Inc.*, a private, not-for-profit health care network serving 16 counties in North Carolina. FirstHealth of the Carolinas is an integrated health care system with a continuum of care that encompasses hospitals, family care centers, school-based clinics, community health, patient transportation, health and fitness centers, and other services – and also an established part of the safety net for vulnerable people in this rural region. Drawing on the resources of its network and partnerships with area agencies, government bodies, churches, and other community entities, FirstHealth Community Voices is focusing on the uninsured and underserved in four rural counties – Moore, Montgomery, Richmond, and Hoke. The population of these counties represents the income disparities and growing diversity of people living in the rural South. Among a relatively affluent, older, white population are African-American communities, pockets of Latinos and Native Americans and Asians, plus low-wage workers, low-income retirees, and unemployed. Many people working in small businesses or on farms in the summer and fall are uninsured.

FirstHealth Community Voices is exploring ways to expand coverage and care to area underserved and communicate lessons and issues with decision makers at the state and national levels. FirstHealth Community Voices established a regional Community Health Board to guide overall project efforts and better connect health system decisions to community interests. FirstConnection is a pilot health care coverage and case management program for uninsured not eligible for other programs. The program is similar to FirstHealth's employee health plan benefit and managed by the same entity. To better track case management across services provided through this rural network, FirstHealth Community Voices also piloted a web-based system called Canopy – technology that is now in demand for use by other systems. Community Voices outreach and enrollment efforts are adding uninsured people to existing programs. To address the oral health needs of uninsured, FirstHealth dental care centers in three counties are expanding services to children and informing practice, health professions training, and policy options in North Carolina.

Northern Manhattan, New York

Northern Manhattan Community Voices represents more than 30 community-based organizations, institutions, and health care providers. Drawn together by core partners – *Alianza Dominicana, Inc., the Columbia University School of Dental and Oral Surgery,* and *Harlem Hospital Center* – partners are working to listen to the underserved and strengthen their voices in health care decision making. Northern Manhattan includes two Manhattan communities – Central Harlem and the Washington Heights-Inwood community. Combined, these two communities represent less than one-third of Manhattan's population, but nearly two-thirds of its Medicaid-eligible. The people in Central Harlem are primarily African American; Washington Heights-Inwood houses New York State's largest Latino community – a mix of Puerto Ricans, Cubans, Mexicans, and Central and South Americans – plus the largest Dominican community in the United States. High rates of poverty, low rates of health insurance coverage, language barriers, public policies that reduce access to care for immigrants – these and other issues impact community health in this culturally diverse part of Manhattan.

Northern Manhattan Community Voices' collaborative partnerships are focused on improving community health and access to health care for the underserved. In addition to sponsoring roundtable discussions and workgroups to address mental health policies and oral health issues, project partners undertake community work to improve health coverage via available programs and expanded care options. Northern Manhattan Community Voices trains community health outreach workers to enroll residents in Medicaid and Child Health Plus, New York's expanded insurance program for children. The project also is coordinating local efforts around disease prevention – spearheading an asthma initiative effort that trains child care providers and parents. Expanded dental health services for low-income elderly are available through the Mannie L. Wilson Senior Center, and dental assistants from Northern Manhattan communities are being trained through a Columbia University program.

Washington, D.C.

The *District of Columbia Department of Health* is home for the District of Columbia Community Voices Collaborative. Made up of health care providers and community-based organizations providing health care to 95 percent of D.C.'s uninsured, Collaborative members are keenly aware of how resource and health care personnel shortages affect community health in the District – especially when compared with the needs of the underserved. More than 81,000 District of Columbia residents are uninsured or underinsured, placing great strain on safety net institutions and services. In the predominantly African-American, D.C. population, 82 percent of the uninsured are single adults. To better coordinate use of resources and draw community perspectives into the development of solutions, the D.C. Community Voices Collaborative is partnering with Department of Health administrations, academic institutions, and local nonprofits to mobilize resources, expand community options for health coverage and access to care, and foster new levels of cooperation among safety net providers.

Acting at times as a convener, a conduit to community perspectives, and a mechanism to consider longstanding health issues and infrastructure problems, the D.C. Community Voices Collaborative has been active in the support and development of a number of health improvement strategies. The D.C. HealthCare Alliance is a public-private partnership to provide health insurance to uninsured residents. Drawing on a network of local hospitals, public health clinics, and primary care providers and specialists, the HealthCare Alliance is open to adults who meet income guidelines and have no health insurance. The D.C. Community Voices Collaborative was involved in the development of the Alliance, and collaborated with the Maternal and Family Health Administration to work through outreach workers to reach eligible enrollees. The D.C. Community Voices Collaborative also has raised the issue of oral health in the District, facilitated the process of establishing standards for oral health assessment, and convened local providers and academic institutions around an oral health assessment process.

West Virginia

The *West Virginia Higher Education Policy Commission, Office of Health Sciences,* the *Governor's Cabinet on Children and Families,* the *LifeBridge, Inc.,* and the *Regional Family Resource Network* are the four lead agencies of the West Virginia Community Voices project. They are joined by 18 partners representing established health coalitions, health professions associations, community health departments, churches, and health providers – seasoned organizations with an interest in the health and well-being of West

Virginians. Many West Virginia residents live in remote, rural areas. Half of all workers have no health insurance coverage, and access to care is further compounded by poverty and transportation issues. Although people of color represent only four percent of the state's population, health disparities among these groups, although often overlooked, are significant. Overall, the health status of West Virginians is among the poorest in the United States with high rates of high blood pressure, diabetes, cancer, and lung disease.

West Virginia Community Voices is focusing on underserved and uninsured in four rural counties – Boon, Clay, Kanawha, and Putnam. Building on the experience and connections of its partner organizations, Community Voices is supporting community action on health and health care issues while it informs state policy discussions about health coverage, care, and related issues. West Virginia Community Voices' efforts contributed to state-level discussions on the design and implementation of West Virginia Children's Health Insurance Program. A Community Voices Oral Health Task Force developed a series of recommendations for oral health care that are informing state policy. Community Voices is partnering with the Regional Family Resource Network to expand community engagement in health care decision making by learning more about issues and challenges facing uninsured and drawing them into the process of developing programs. By including underserved in deliberations and discussions, and publishing a report on minority health issues, West Virginia Community Voices laid the groundwork for formally addressing minority health issues by partnering with state agencies to establish a Minority Health Program within the state infrastructure.

While each Community Voices site is a distinct partnership with its own set of partners, ways of working, and targets, their work has taken aim at particular challenges and identified some workable strategies for addressing access and coverage issues, oral health, and more. The next several chapters look across the Community Voices programs to identify examples of products or processes at work and clarify lessons with broad implications for policy and practice.

Chapter 3:
Expanding Access to Health Coverage and Community Care

- *A self-employed cab driver in New York City* is willing to pay for a doctor visit if he is sick, but he does not understand why he should buy health insurance coverage. Born in the Dominican Republic, the idea of paying for something you might need in the future does not make sense to him. He'd rather save his money now and envisions paying installments over time if he should need some expensive medical treatment.

- The *laid-off construction worker* carries four worn slips of paper in his wallet – prescriptions he hasn't been able to fill since his job ended. Sitting across from him in the clinic waiting room, another man without coverage explains how he makes health care decisions. "If it isn't life-threatening, and it isn't going to kill you," he says, "give it a few days and it might go away." –as reported in *The Baltimore Sun*

- An Asian woman nods in agreement about the importance of coverage for her daughter, a child with chronic asthma who qualifies for Children's Health Insurance Program (CHIP) coverage in California. But she *has no doctor herself* – and no way to get one without health coverage. Plus, she is busy running her business and taking care of her daughter – too busy to worry about herself.

- "When I tried to refer a patient to an ear, nose, and throat physician, I could not get them in for three months. When I call personally and beg and plead, they make it two months. They are just too busy. If you need something acutely – if you have a car accident – you will be taken care of immediately. But if you have *a chronic disease that simply needs to be managed – diabetes or asthma* – you will have a hard time getting in to see a physician even if you have insurance." –New Mexico M.D. talking about health personnel shortages on a local radio show

- A man who once had health coverage and steady income now finds himself opening *collection agency letters*. In need of acute care and outpatient services after he became a crime victim, he was unable to work during his recovery, *lost his insurance*, and now finds his life on a different path.

- "I lost a good friend to diabetes," says one minister. "I was working with him as usual on Friday, and by Monday, he was in the hospital. He had *no idea he had diabetes*."

For people without health coverage, access to health care services is limited. Without a payment mechanism in place, most uninsured delay seeking health care until an emergency arises. The result often is avoidable health problems, lost productivity, unnecessary suffering, and greater cost – to individuals and their families, to health care providers, and to people who pay taxes and health premiums.

With or without insurance, the culture of health systems is difficult to understand and harder to navigate.

Even for those with coverage, access may be limited or fraught with tension and conflict. With or without insurance, the culture of health systems is difficult to understand and harder to navigate. And for those who speak a different language or who must travel great distances for care, for people of color who seldom see others from their communities providing care in health systems, the barriers to access are many and complicated.

Financial, Geographic, and Cultural Barriers to Access

The most widely recognized obstacle to health care access is lack of health coverage. With the number of uninsured hovering around 40 million, the U.S. Census Bureau estimates almost half of workers with incomes at or below the poverty level have no health coverage. But Community Voices projects have learned that coverage is only one determinant of whether people can or will seek the services they need.

With or without coverage, cost is often a barrier to accessing health services. Among people with few resources, fear of "what it

38

might cost" – in terms of payment for services, lost work, time and trouble to family members – keeps many underserved people from finding out if the lump or cough or pain is something serious. People with chronic health problems (asthma, diabetes, high blood pressure, heart problems) may seek crisis care for years before the root cause of an illness is properly identified.

For some who might be eligible for Medicaid or local indigent care programs, a fear of being stigmatized as "too poor" or "a charity case" is a deterrent. Many working people proud of their independence will flinch at the suggestion that they visit a social services office. Others who might be receptive to available coverage options may not be aware that they would qualify for Medicaid or other programs. People who have recently come to the United States – to work or join family members – may be fearful about accessing health systems in general. Worried that they might be labeled a "public charge," many immigrants who need care avoid public hospitals and free clinics except in cases of dire emergency.

Barriers to access vary according to a community's needs and situation.

Feelings of intimidation may be another barrier to accessing needed health services. Low-income families, immigrants who do not speak English easily, people who come from different life experiences and cultures – all of these may find the routine questions and patterns of care in health systems daunting. Barriers to access vary according to a community's needs and situation. Language is a serious obstacle for non-English speakers. Yet even in municipalities with large non-English speaking populations, few medical offices, clinics, and hospitals can afford to retain qualified medical translators on staff or provide written materials in many languages.

Traditional Systems Present Hidden Barriers

A clinic or medical office's hours of operation may unwittingly create another obstacle to accessing routine health care services. Hours may be too limited for low-income workers and others with little flexibility in their schedules. In communities with provider shortages, long waiting times at clinics and even longer waits for appointments make it difficult for some to access care via existing services. Lack of transportation or child care and other logistical difficulties can present insurmountable barriers for people of color, immigrants, low-income workers, and other underserved.

The way services are offered also may discourage people from accessing services. People who receive insensitive care or confusing directions shy away from returning for more – and most likely tell family and friends about their experiences. For others, what they *need* is not what they get. Underserved people know they can walk into an emergency room if they are bleeding, but their most pressing needs may be dental care or treatment for mental health issues. The health systems providing care to vulnerable communities may not be aware of priorities like these. And even if they are, most safety net providers, already working with limited resources, are hard pressed to expand services without funding streams.

Mental health, oral health, and preventative care (such as routine physical exams, mammograms, and so on) are not generally reimbursable as part of primary care. To provide these "extras" to uninsured and underserved populations, health systems, clinics, and other safety net providers must piece together funding from assorted state and federal programs and/or grants. But cobbling together even a short-term program takes time, manpower, and expertise – three ingredients in short supply for most safety net providers.

Community Voices Sparks Dialogue to Identify Health Needs and Values

Well aware of these and other challenges, Community Voices projects have set their sights on finding ways both to expand access to health care for the underserved and to pay for it in a highly competitive marketplace. In doing so, they target more than health coverage. They seek viable ways to reshape existing systems and make better use of resources with the overall goal of making their communities healthier. Recognizing that each community health delivery system is unique and rests on a complicated set of assumptions and practices, Community Voices participants turn their systems upside down to examine things from a different perspective.

They start with the people they seek to serve, to understand the dynamics of the systems in place, likely pressure points, and unlikely connections. Who are the uninsured and underserved in their communities? How do they define health? What do they need from health delivery systems? What do they value? How do they use the current systems – and why or why not? Community Voices is answering these questions first, actively engaging uninsured and those typically on the outside of health care decision making in the discussion. For example:

In Miami, Florida, Community Voices public forums invited people to share their perspectives on health, local systems, and community issues. Held in city neighborhoods and nearby migrant worker communities, more than 600 consumers using local safety net systems shared their experiences and expressed their frustrations. The videotaped remarks – often made in Spanish and translated – formed the basis of a community report and carry a potent message to decision makers in local health systems.

In Northern Manhattan, surveys and focus groups with beauty salon employees, livery cab drivers, and other small business employees found that, although most do not have health coverage, they are paying for care. This information has become the basis for a small business product in development – a health coverage option tailored to the needs of two- and three-person businesses.

In Baltimore, Maryland; Washington, D.C.; and across West Virginia, Community Voices participants have engaged in the same process – listening intently and letting what they hear build a foundation for Community Voices efforts. Often the information gleaned at the community level has shaped the process by which additional data is collected and shared. In Alameda County, California, for example, Community Voices focus groups led to the development of a major survey of uninsured conducted in seven different languages.

These forums, surveys, focus groups, and other efforts to reach people in communities help clarify who is underserved in distinct communities. Community Voices partners in Northern Manhattan, Baltimore, Miami, and West Virginia have been able to confirm that a large proportion of the uninsured in their communities are working people. In fact, Community Voices sites are finding that seasonal workers, construction laborers, low-wage workers, and employees of small businesses make up a significant share of those without ready access to coverage and care. In many Community Voices communities, this information is broadening the vision of health system and community decision makers. Rather than a

41

faceless target population, the uninsured became people working and living in their communities.

At the same time, Community Voices projects draw provider communities into the dialogue – fostering personal connections that lay the groundwork for a common understanding. Providers, many of whom feel frustrated with the limitations of existing systems, have many insights and ideas to bring to bear on system limitations. Yet they often have little interaction with members of underserved communities except in emergency rooms or clinics. Others with perspectives on community needs and desires – ministers, advocacy groups, employers, schools, neighborhood organizations – are joining discussions as well. The collective view of this array of health system stakeholders has prompted the exploration and development of some very community-specific solutions to coverage and access.

The solutions they engender suggest a range of possibilities for other communities.

In Washington, D.C., Community Voices has been instrumental in the development and nurturing of a public-private partnership to expand access to care for uninsured residents. The Department of Health's D.C. Health Care Alliance creates a community provider network linking three hospitals, six public health clinics, and nearly 750 primary care providers and specialists. To make certain that the uninsured D.C. residents most in need would receive accurate information about the new program, teams of community outreach workers move throughout the district talking to people; making presentations at churches and PTA meetings; and stopping at coin laundries, barber shops, and beauty salons. To date, thanks to outreach and provider collaboration across the community, more than 26,000 low-income people are enrolled in the program.

What works in Washington, D.C., may not be possible in Iowa or Georgia or Maine. But taken together, Community Voices sites reflect the diversity of the United States as a whole – many-layered urban communities and remote rural areas; communities with large immigrant populations or made up primarily of Indian people; areas that are health resource rich as well as those with severe shortages of personnel, facilities, and financial reserves. As one Community Voices leader notes, "Because of the very diverseness of our population, one solution will not work across the country." The solutions they engender suggest a range of possibilities for other communities – ways to surmount access barriers and expand coverage to encompass more people – in many cases, thousands of uninsured and underserved typically on the fringes of the health care marketplace.

Certainly, products from Community Voices work to date vary according to community needs, policy climates, readiness, and resources. But there are common elements – perspectives emerging in El Paso and New York and Denver and Colorado – that are fueling Community Voices pursuits nationwide.

Community Voices: Community Care vs. Medical Care

Community Voices is building models that encompass services beyond medical care. And rather than focus only on coverage issues, Community Voices projects are looking at the community as a whole, identifying access barriers that include lack of coverage. Using survey data, case studies, stories, videotaped remarks, public meetings, and other tools to uncover community perceptions, Community Voices is helping identify and explain how barriers to access affect community health and the flow of health system resources. Together, Community Voices confirms that access and coverage are inextricably linked. As one Community Voices leader intones, "You can't expand one without the other. They belong together."

Creating a Health Commons
UNM Care Plan, Community Voices New Mexico

The UNM Care Plan is a model that manages both the cost and care of approximately 15,000 uninsured and underserved people in Bernalillo County, New Mexico. Through Community Voices Shared Solutions, the University of New Mexico (UNM) Health Sciences Center took the lead to work with safety net providers countywide to expand access to primary care services for the uninsured and community site-based case management. An inclusive planning process helped surface and address the concerns of institutional and community stakeholders in the development of the plan. "The UNM Care model creates a primary care home for the uninsured and seeks to reduce costs and improve quality of care to the underserved," explains Dan Derksen, director of the University's Center for Community Partnerships. The plan invests in long-term patient-provider relationships and a greater focus on preventative services to reduce costs over time.

Uninsured county residents who enter the program receive primary care serves from one of the ten UNM-run clinics or five First Choice Community Health clinics in and around Albuquerque. Participants do not pay a monthly premium, but assume responsibility for co-payments for doctor visits, tests, medications, and urgent care services. To document the process and provide information to safety net institutions and community stakeholders, data are collected on enrollees, and use of services tracked. Results from the first two years of operations reported in an article in *Academic Medicine* (April 2000) indicate that managing the care of uninsured patients can reduce utilization as well as cost and better meet the needs of uninsured and underserved populations.

"At the hub of this community-based approach is the 'health commons' – a method for pooling resources from public and private entities to address complex health issues within the community that cannot be solved by one entity alone," Derksen explains. "It's not a biomedical model but a different operational approach – community-based, primary care sites that include medical, social, dental, and case management services."

In New Mexico, county governments are responsible for managing funds and services for indigent care programs. The UNM Care Plan pools county funds from property taxes, federal match for disproportionate share (DSH) dollars, Medicaid sole community provider support, public health, and other funds with UNM and health clinic resources. To broaden access to the program, facilitate enrollment, and handle the increased demand for primary care the plan would create, UNM's School of Medicine hired 12 new primary care physician faculty and five family nurse practitioners, extended clinic hours, and expanded hospital staff support in the primary care clinics.

The UNM Care Plan not only creates "co-locations" for primary care, but prompts new levels of collaboration among providers and redirects health care resources. Wayne Powell, associate director of the Center for Community Partnerships, says UNM Care Plan efforts in one county are changing relationships and creating new ways of expanding the safety net infrastructure in New Mexico. "As the state's only academic health center, the University of New Mexico brings resources and credibility to the process," Powell acknowledges. "But we face barriers common to academic and other health systems." Derksen agrees adding, "The system we're trying to set up is primary care. Reimbursement within the medical center is aligned with tertiary care services. Payments for emergency and intensive care services create fiscal incentives for resisting change. When resources are scarce, decentralized primary care systems can be seen as a threat."

Powell and Derksen credit creating a broad-based understanding of issues as the factor that made it possible for providers to overcome natural skepticism and commit to the UNM Care Plan. Arthur Kaufman, M.D., chair of the Department of Family and Community Medicine, explains how the program is shaping the educational mission of the University: "The great majority of patients enrolled in our Family Practice residents' panels are UNM Care patients. Because these patients are managed, residents receive data on their practice and learn principles of managed care every day in clinic." Data gathered also provides information to help guide future decisions about services and allocation of resources.

"A Sight to Behold"
Ingham Health Plan, Ingham Community Voices

Community Voices work stresses the importance of creating a common community understanding of health issues and priorities. In Ingham County, Community Voices has pursued that strategy to spark collaboration around the development of an organized system of care. "The collaboration represents a quantum leap," according to Chuck Steinberg, contract manager for Ingham County and current president of the Ingham Health Plan Corporation Board. "We've gone from something that many people thought was a noble idea we might see 'in the next life' to a working process that is a sight to behold." The Ingham Community Voices effort that began with interviews of key stakeholders expanded to encompass forums across the county and resulted in a tangible action plan that draws on a wide base of financial and other community resources. Ingham Health Plan (IHP) is one key element of the overall action agenda.

The broad-spectrum effort is improving health care access to more than 14,000 of the county's uninsured.

IHP is a community-sponsored program that offers primary care; specialty care; and outpatient laboratory, x-ray, and pharmacy services to low-income people in Ingham County not eligible for Medicaid, Medicare, or other programs. Community engagement has been an essential part of shaping the benefit package and determining where and how to use resources.

> *"Some would advise you to find the 'power people' to solve a problem. Community Voices is the opposite approach."*
>
> —*Bruce Bragg, Ingham County*

"When IHP began," Steinberg recalls, "there was an interest among providers to include an inpatient benefit. But consumers said, 'We represent a group of people who have to decide between clothing and food for our kids and medical care for ourselves!' That kind of insight took IHP in a different direction. Instead of limiting the number of people and including hospitalization, IHP developed an outpatient services package that would reach more than 14,000 who were without coverage."

Ingham Health Department Director Bruce Bragg believes the systematic, inclusive engagement process Ingham Community Voices undertook has won over skeptics about the value of throwing a wide net. "Some would advise you to find the 'power people' to solve a problem. Community Voices is the opposite approach," he says. "We engage lots of people and put deeper roots into the community to sustain and expand the work."

Ingham Community Voices has led to the creation of a prescription program for a three-county area that is being replicated in 17 Michigan counties. Marketing to reach Ingham County uninsured is increasing awareness of IHP and increasing applications for Medicaid and Healthy Kids (Michigan's CHIP program). As community needs become better understood, other programs are in the works. Because so many uninsured in the area are low-income workers or people employed by small businesses, Ingham Community Voices is developing a Small Employers Subsidy Program to expand health insurance coverage in this growing market.

Chuck Steinberg is optimistic about the future of IHP. "The IHP funding mechanism took county dollars, added federal match, and is increasing the resource base – making it possible to take what was in place through the health department and build enhancements," says Steinberg. "IHP puts a card in the hands of people who were uninsured and connects them to a well-organized process of care." Steinberg sees the impact of Community Voices on coverage and access issues as far-reaching. "Having the collective voices of the community heard," he says, "building collaborative bridges between groups, and trying innovative approaches that never would have been attempted are the results of our efforts so far."

Service-Driven Care
Turtle Health Plan, California Rural Indian Health Board (CRIHB)

Turtle Health Plan is the first statewide health maintenance organization created by and for American Indians. When it begins enrolling members sometime in 2003, Turtle will join the primary care resources of 21 Indian health programs in 36 California counties and represent the participation of 69 distinct tribes. Enrollment of tribal members is expected to exceed 20,000, and members will have the benefit of seamless care that extends from primary care clinics to a network of contracts with specialists and other providers.

"Turtle will answer to tribal communities and represent a commitment to improve the health status of its members."
—Andy Anderson, CRIHB

The scope and reach of the organization alone would make it unique. But CRIHB's Andy Anderson says the differences between Turtle Health Plan and other HMOs will run deeper. "Turtle will be service-driven," he explains. "For-profit insurance companies need to answer to investors, but Turtle will answer to tribal communities and represent a commitment to improve the health status of its members." This service-driven focus is built on an understanding of the roles and responsibilities of sovereign tribes and a keen awareness of the shortcomings of existing service delivery models for Indian people.

Tribal governments have the rights and responsibilities of state and federal entities, but severe limitations on their ability to marshal resources to meet those responsibilities. Some tribes in California are large and located near health care facilities, but others have few members and are located far away from clinics or hospitals. Despite these differences, all share common problems of poverty, unemployment, and chronic health issues such as diabetes and alcoholism. Existing systems, Anderson admits, have few incentives for improving the health of Indian people. "Indian Health Services, S-CHIP, and other programs pay their rate whether you get better or not," he says.

CRIHB Executive Director Jim Crouch believes the Turtle Health Plan departs from these approaches in some fundamental ways. "Turtle will close the loop on information and services. The plan will require analysis of experiences in clinics so changes to improve services and control costs will be made," he says. "We will send utilization data by cost and diagnosis to clinics on a monthly basis," Anderson adds. "Clinics don't get that data now." In addition, connections between primary and other providers will be strengthened to ensure culturally-appropriate care, improve communication, and streamline the transfer of information. The California Department of Health Services has been involved in the development of Turtle Health Plan in part because of its potential to better address the health issues of Native American people. In an interview with the *Sacramento Business Journal*, Gail Margolis, deputy director chief of Medi-Cal, commented, "We're working closely with the Turtle Health Plan to help them develop their proposal. We recognize that this population is underserved."

The basis of the Turtle Health Plan is the network of 21 Indian Health Programs and the guidance of the Turtle board of directors with representation from each of the tribes committed to participating. Crouch and Anderson believe the strides in developing the model to date are the result of an intensive education process that has engaged both clinic staff and tribal leaders. As tribal leaders learn about the potential of Turtle Health Plan to improve the health and well-being of their people and increase the level of community involvement in the process, Turtle is attracting new participants. "I was very skeptical when I first looked at this HMO concept," says Molin Malicay, executive director of Sonoma County Indian Health and chair of the Turtle Health Plan board of directors. "But now I am truly convinced that this model will further expand the health of the native people in California." As Crouch explains, "The community focus will change what services are provided. Over time, Turtle Health Plan will allow for investments that focus on seeing impact in population health."

Community Voices: Strengthening Fragile Infrastructures

Access issues are often symptoms of infrastructure problems – lack of needed facilities, personnel, or funding; missing connections between existing services; allocation of resources out of line with community needs or woefully inadequate; a confusing regulatory or policy climate that rewards competition over scare resources rather than collaboration. Community Voices efforts to expand health care access and coverage for underserved populations are highlighting the value of a stronger health services delivery infrastructure to better meet community needs – and identifying methods for shoring up shaky systems.

"Sticking Together"
Primary Care Plan, Community Voices El Paso

"El Paso is the number one major metropolitan area of uninsured in the nation," Pete Duarte of Thomason General Hospital says flatly. "The fourth poorest metro area and third poorest zip code in the U.S., a medical manpower shortage area, and the gateway to the north for thousands of immigrants from Mexico. In other words," he concludes with a wry understatement, "we don't have a whole lot of resources." With 70,000 uninsured and an unrelenting drain on already pressed safety net providers, Community Voices El Paso brought together the nonprofit community to find a way to address these issues. "We determined that if we were going to make any impact, we needed to stick together," Duarte recalls. John Romero, executive director for Centro San Vincente, a federally qualified health center, and an active Community Voices participant, agrees. "Community Voices gathered both common and competing interests among service providers. It has provided a framework for beginning to look at how – together – we can better impact service needs and resource allocation."

Through Community Voices efforts, the group created El Paso's Primary Health Plan. "Some people thought we were throwing good money after bad by investing in the Plan," Duarte adds. "But we just about broke even in our second year and next year will see return on our investment." Duarte says "sticking together" has been the key, and many partners have had a role in making the

Primary Health Plan a workable program. "It cost between $6 and $8 million to get the HMO up and running," he admits, but that is only one dimension of making the Plan effective. More than 400 local providers are part of the network of primary care and specialist physicians providing services through the Plan. And El Paso community-based organizations are handling enrollment for the coverage while Community Voices provides training to expedite the application process. "The ongoing training and focus groups that are part of this process are essential," Duarte says emphatically.

Bill Schlesinger, co-director for Project Vida and a Community Voices participant, believes the Plan changes the orientation of funding for indigent community members in a fundamental way. "Previously, dollars for indigent care were allocated directly to the providers," Schlesinger explains. "This model changes the norm in that the health care dollars follow the client, and the client has a choice about where those primary care dollars are spent."

El Paso, like many provider and nonprofit communities, has its turf issues. Duarte calls it a "keep it here" perspective – the desire to keep resources within established institutions. But he and others note a ground shift in El Paso among providers, some political leaders, and a great many of Community Voices El Paso's partners – a desire to build a community network that will provide better care for underserved in El Paso. "Previously, the focus was trying to make resources go as far as possible," says Duarte. "Community Voices has been the spark to try to develop an integrated delivery health care network to change how things are done." In the meantime, more than 7,000 previously uninsured are now enrolled in El Paso's Primary Health Plan – people who would not be eligible for Medicaid or other programs.

Rebuilding a Foundation "Piece by Piece"
Voices of Detroit Initiative (VODI)

The Voices of Detroit Initiative (VODI) has developed a "virtual system" of care for uninsured city residents. "There is no premium, no insurance provider," VODI's Lucille Smith says. "But VODI represents an organized system of care for uninsured who do not qualify for other programs." Each person enrolled in VODI is assigned to a provider and a system that links primary care providers with local hospitals. Overall, VODI reflects collaboration among Detroit's major health care systems and federally qualified health clinics. But the arrangement that marries tertiary care and primary care is nowhere near as simple as it may sound.

"Resources have been depleted in Detroit," Smith explains. "We have no public hospital system, and the hospitals providing secondary and tertiary care, for the most part, did not have primary care. The question becomes not only how to provide primary care for the uninsured, but who gets paid for providing it?" In answering that question, Smith says that VODI partners are working to provide services based on the needs of Detroit residents and build collaborative connections to link traditional competitors. "For our community, it had to be done," she admits. "Solving the problem of the uninsured is a common problem for our partners. For many reasons, our resources were limited."

More than 7,600 people are enrolled in VODI – over 70 percent of the working people with no other access to health coverage.

Yet even with limited resources, VODI partners are creating medical homes for uninsured, tracking system use, and expanding care options for Detroit's underserved. More than 7,600 people are enrolled in the VODI virtual system – and over 70 percent of these are working people with no other access to health coverage. Henry Ford Health System's James Chesney identifies that as one of the big surprises of VODI's collaborative efforts. "We continue to find that the biggest unanticipated benefit of VODI has been the placement of people into existing programs – Michigan's Plus Care and Medicaid," Chesney observes. "When we started, we believed that we would need to provide insurance for the uninsured ourselves. Now we are finding we are able to link people up with other programs."

Coordination and cooperation among providers are crucial, VODI partners agree. According to Sister Mary E. Howard of Detroit's Cabrini Clinic: "VODI forced communication between competing parties to address community needs. This communication has been the springboard for other collaborative initiatives." Vernice Davis Anthony of St. John Health System concurs, adding that collaboration is expanding resources for Detroit's safety net systems. "HRSA (the federal Health Resources Service Administration) has assured us that they are very willing to bring significant new primary care dollars to Detroit as long as we continue to work together," Anthony says.

The Detroit Medical Center's John B. Waller, Jr., acknowledges, "The process is not necessarily easy. However, if a community stays focused and persistent, there are a variety of benefits that accrue both internal to the collaborating partners and external to the intended beneficiaries." As Lucille Smith concludes, "VODI is building a system using the parts we have to build a whole – rebuilding the foundation piece by piece."

Increasing Awareness, Streamlining Enrollment
Denver Health Facilitated Enrollment Program,
Denver Health Community Voices

Denver Health CEO and Medical Director Patricia A. Gabow relates lack of coverage to community health issues – both for uninsured people and the institutions that serve them. "An uninsured child is 80 percent more likely never to get routine health care," she wrote in a *Denver Rocky Mountain News* viewpoint. "And more than half of uninsured adults have no regular source of health care." For public hospital systems in urban areas, this often translates into a crippling financial burden that erodes institutional viability. Denver Health was no stranger to this kind of pressure. According to Gabow, "Denver Health provided more than $212 million of care to uninsured people in 2001 – 40 percent of all our charges, 42 percent of all unsponsored care in the Denver area, and 30 percent of all unsponsored care in the state."

Community Voices made it possible for the development and piloting of AppTrack, an enrollment tracking system.

To address the uninsured issue, Gabow says Community Voices collaboration made it possible to redouble efforts to reach those eligible for Medicaid and the Children's Health Insurance Plan (CHIP) – to raise awareness and reduce enrollment obstacles for Denver's uninsured. "We reasoned that if we could enroll everyone who is eligible for Medicaid and CHIP, individuals and the community would be healthier, and the new revenues would permit us to develop a better system of care for the uninsured," she says. Through surveys of area uninsured and other methods,

Community Voices determined that many did not know about available programs. Drawing together social services providers, area nonprofits, and neighborhood organizations, Denver Health Community Voices is partnering with more than 200 community organizations to reach uninsured populations. Six full-time community outreach workers and a corps of trained Medicaid and CHIP enrollment workers link with partner organizations and help streamline access to coverage. In one year alone, the program resulted in 52,000 new applications for Medicaid and CHIP programs for uninsured community members.

As part of an overall focus on finding and enrolling Denver's uninsured, Community Voices made it possible for the development and piloting of AppTrack, an enrollment tracking system. AppTrack is now a tool Denver Health uses, as well as the Denver Department of Human Services, Colorado's Medicaid managed care organization, and the statewide community health network.

"Community Voices ... has made a difference in the way we operate."

—Elizabeth Whitley, Denver

As an integrated delivery system that provides primary care through a network of neighborhood clinics and public health services, Denver Health delivers primary, secondary, and tertiary care services. But Elizabeth Whitley of Denver Health Community Voices says, "Integrating care across providers is a challenge we are addressing. Co-morbidity – problems with physical health, mental health, and substance abuse issues – is so common. Traditionally, those services are in 'silos' that separate care for physical health from mental health and substance abuse treatment." Case management is helping underserved community members access care within Denver Health. Case management data and stories are identifying system gaps and fostering cooperation across traditional "silos" of care.

Whitley notes that responses to a survey of Denver Health Community Voices partners pointed to the strength of these connections and the value of collaboration. She sees changes in Denver Health too. "In the past, we looked inside Denver Health to make the institution healthier," she remembers. "Community Voices made us look to the community. It put us out there where people are and has made a difference in the way we operate."

One Step at a Time
FirstConnection, FirstHealth Community Voices, North Carolina

Felton Capel, FirstHealth Community Health board chairman, sees FirstConnection as an entrée to expanding coverage for the uninsured. "We knew that the problem of the large number of uninsured in our area would not be one that was remedied quickly," he says thoughtfully. "We've taken things one step at a time, working to develop solutions." Step one for FirstHealth Community Voices was to raise awareness and enroll those eligible in available programs including Medicaid. "As gaps in eligibility emerged, our work began," Capel says. "FirstConnection was designed to assist the population left out of government programs. It is a product designed to provide affordable coverage for those who earn too much to receive public assistance, but who are still unable to afford private health insurance."

FirstConnection offers health care services and case management for eligible uninsured adults and children. A subsidized program, FirstConnection is administered by the same health maintenance organization that administers FirstHealth employee benefits. With modest co-payments, the coverage provides preventive services, primary care, specialist care, and inpatient hospital care as well as mental health services and prescription drug coverage. Enrollees receive physicals, health screening services, and an initial physician visit as part of the enrollment process. Education to manage chronic disease conditions such as diabetes is part of the case management.

As a pilot program, the number of participants has been modest (200 at the outset). But the pilot is providing baseline information about the costs of covering previously uninsured community members. Lisa Hartsock of FirstHealth Community Voices says the data from the initial two years of FirstConnection is promising. "The overall cost of caring for this uninsured population is not as high as previously projected," she explains. "On average, the utilization patterns and the overall cost mirror that of the commercially insured population."

Case management makes it possible to monitor care for enrollees and assist with scheduling physician appointments, transportation, and related support services participants might require. The development of innovative case management software is making it possible for FirstHealth to collect data on utilization and cost more efficiently system-wide. Another positive outgrowth of FirstConnection is a subsidized insurance product for small businesses under development. FirstPlan, as the product is named, will be piloted in Moore County, targeting the small businesses that together employ more than 3,000 uninsured. This uninsured group sought services last year that resulted in $2.3 million in uncompensated care. "We are learning as we go with these programs," Felton Capel believes. "And we plan to keep pressing forward with our efforts."

FirstHealth President and CEO Charles T. Frock refers to approaches like these as "recognizing the obvious." As he explains, "Whether you're a single system serving a rural population, such as FirstHealth, or a collaboration of safety net providers in an urban area, you already *are* taking care of everyone." His advice to health systems and safety net providers is to do the right thing and the prudent thing: "Step up, declare your commitment, and develop an organized way to deliver care in a cost-effective manner."

Community Voices: Envisioning Health Care for All

While expanded Medicaid and CHIP coverage, reallocation of resources, pilot projects, and intensive outreach and enrollment connect some uninsured with access to coverage and care, many others remain outside of systems by virtue of their income, residency, family grouping, or immigration status. Low-income adults without dependent children and undocumented immigrant adults and children are among those most often left out of even innovative approaches to expand coverage and care. In targeting underserved, Community Voices has come up against these barriers many times and continue to explore ways to overcome health system and policy obstacles. Some models described above or in the following chapters illustrate approaches to building systems to address the needs of a particular underserved group. But at the heart of these efforts is a conviction that health care for people regardless of their group, income, or residency status should be a right – not unlike the public education of school children. This vision is driving the development of broad-based Community Voices models like one in Alameda County, California.

Not Marginal, but Central
Alliance Family Care, Alameda County, California

Sherry Hirota, CEO of Asian Health Services in Oakland, California, knows immigrant health is not a marginal issue. The residents of Alameda County's largest city and surrounding area include large African-American, Asian, and Latino populations. Among these are dozens of ethnic groups representing Korean, Vietnamese, Chinese, Filipino, Mexican, Central American, and other immigrants. "You cannot address the uninsured without addressing immigrant issues," she believes. Hirota and Jane Garcia, her counterpart at La Clinica de La Raza, live this dictum. The two combined have to their credit almost a half century's activism around the provision of health care to underserved immigrant populations. This breadth and depth of experience lend great credibility to both the community-based health services delivery organizations they lead in Alameda County and the Oakland Community Voices collaboration to expand health care to underserved and uninsured residents.

Garcia and Hirota, along with the Alameda Health Consortium, an association of nonprofit community health centers, share the responsibility for guiding Oakland Community Voices. Tomiko Connor, Oakland's project director, says: "Often community-based organizations are looked to for information 'on the ground' but not to lead. The fact that these community-based organizations are immigrant-focused – not viewing immigrants as a 'special population' but a central population – with credibility in the community and relationships in place has been important. People provide the glue and the impetus for this work."

Oakland Community Voices is one of the key partners in the Alameda County Access to Care Collaborative, a group comprised of the leadership of the Alameda Alliance for Health, the Alameda County Health Care Services Agency, the Alameda County Medical Center, the Alameda County Social Services Agency, and the Alameda Health Consortium. Irene Ibarra, CEO of Alameda Alliance for Health, believes that the Oakland Community Voices "umbrella" makes ongoing collaboration possible. "We are constantly – daily, it seems – going back to that collaborative base for thinking, conceptualization, program implementation, and resources," she says.

Alameda Alliance for Health is a nonprofit, managed care plan serving approximately 80,000 Alameda County residents. Alliance members receive health care services from a network of providers – more than 1,300 area physicians, 15 hospitals, 26 community health centers, and at least 170 pharmacies. In partnership with Oakland Community Voices, the Alliance developed and launched Alliance Family Care, a subsidized health care coverage product for low-income parents and children. Families pay monthly premiums based on their income and receive medical, dental, prescription, mental health, family planning, chiropractic, acupuncture, and maternity care services through Alliance Family Care. "It's an investment in prevention services," Ibarra offers to explain how Family Care differs from other products. "It is dental care and screenings and prenatal care – the things working families told us in focus groups that they needed and were willing to pay for." Initially, the Alliance allocated $4.1 million of their reserve funds for Family Care. Since that time, the allocation has been increased to almost $15 million and leveraged support from other sources, including the county, The California Endowment, and the California HealthCare Foundation.

"You cannot address the uninsured without addressing immigrant issues."

—Sherry Hirota,
Alameda County

The tremendous investment in Alliance Family Care illustrates the extent of the need for expanded care and coverage in Alameda County. Nearly 16 percent of adults in the county are uninsured – three-quarters of these, people of color, and a majority are immigrants or of immigrant heritage. The intention behind Family Care is to extend coverage to low-income families who do not qualify for other coverage programs – and to do so regardless of immigration status. Since the summer of 2000, more than 6,000 have been enrolled in the program. One-third of the enrollees are children; more than half speak Spanish as their primary language and almost 20 percent speak Cantonese.

At the same time Alliance Family Care was launched to begin addressing the uninsured problem in Alameda County, Oakland Community Voices joined with the county of Alameda and the Alameda Alliance for Health to sponsor the County of Alameda Uninsured Survey (CAUS). CAUS is the first multi-language, county-specific survey to gather data on uninsured adults. "The survey supplements existing data on children," Connor explains.

"It also provides crucial baseline data to help us understand the state of the uninsured from July through October 2000." Connor envisions this as a periodic assessment, but in the meantime, the data is fueling dialogue about uninsured and providing impetus and support for additional options.

Using data from the survey, the Alameda County Access to Care Collaborative developed a proposal for universal health care coverage that was submitted to the County Board of Supervisors in late 2001. Group Care, another subsidized, managed care product launched in 2001 – this one for in-home supportive service workers – is administered by the Alameda Alliance for Health as well. Other collaborative efforts – around the provision of language support for community clinics, outreach, and enrollment – are in process.

One notable collaboration occurred when the group came together to deliver a single message about the allocation of funds from the state's tobacco settlement. "With millions of dollars on the table, the usual approach would be individual organizations positioning themselves for a portion of the amount," Sherry Hirota explains. "But we all came together and said, 'What the county needs most is to expand coverage to uninsured.'" Hirota considers activities like these as evidence of timely collaboration fostered by Community Voices. "By coming together, we adopted a strategy that benefits all of us instead of 'wedge politics,'" says Hirota. "Our core strategy is to stick to a comprehensive approach."

Chapter 4:
Placing Oral Health Care
Within Reach of the Underserved

- *"I've already lost three teeth because I couldn't pay for a root canal...It's hard to admit, but sometimes we don't have a dollar for a soda let alone $1,000 for a root canal."* –Woman in her 20s speaking at a Miami meeting

- *"Kids sit in class with their heads in their hands because of a toothache."* –Principal of an elementary school in Northern Manhattan

- *"The closest oral health provider is 80 miles away. That's almost 8,000 people with no access to dental care of any kind."* –New Mexico dentist talking about the need for a clinic in a rural community

- *"Data indicate that the extent of decay in children is inversely related to income level."* –Allan J. Formicola, D.D.S, Dean, Columbia University School of Dental and Oral Surgery

- In West Virginia, only half of residents receive regular dental care and almost that same percentage of elderly lose all or most of their teeth.

- In one Midwestern community with 225 dentists, less than 15 percent regularly submit Medicaid claims – and of these, only one is known to routinely accept Medicaid patients.

Americans are recognized the world over for their perfect smiles – and with good reason. Advances in dental science have all but eliminated the need for suffering from dental cavities, and orthodontia and cosmetic dentistry make it possible for many with less-than-perfect teeth to acquire them. But for too many – working poor, uninsured, people of color, and immigrants among them – advances in dental care and treatment are far out of reach. Lacking insurance coverage or the means to pay for services, many low-income people say that cost is the greatest barrier to oral health care. For others – rural residents, people with Medicaid coverage, low-income workers, and immigrants in urban areas – finding a dentist to provide care is a bigger challenge.

Only about 40 percent of people in the United States have some form of dental coverage. For the rest, regular dental visits are an out-of-pocket expense. In most middle class families with or without dental insurance, a visit to the dentist for regular cleanings and check-ups is routine. In households functioning closer to the survival level, seeking dental care is less frequent and often related to pain or other symptoms of a problem. Community Voices program leaders believe the differences in patterns of oral health care are symptomatic of larger issues confronting people as they try to access systems to meet their health needs.

Unacceptable Discrepancies and Disproportionate Gains

Without question, oral health issues relate to overall health and well-being. Regular oral health care makes it possible to avoid gum disease and oral infections, and detect many life-threatening diseases – oral and throat cancers, diabetes, HIV/AIDS – in the early stages. In the absence of oral health care, pain, infection, loss of teeth, and gum disease are the norm and related health consequences often are unavoidable. Gum disease and oral infections may pave the way for preterm birth, heart disease, and stroke. And for people who smoke or have diabetes, the risks are greater. Unfortunately, for communities with large underserved populations, lack of oral health care often translates into more serious illness requiring more expensive treatment with less chance of restoring health as a result.

Lack of oral health care often translates into more serious illness requiring more expensive treatment.

The people most at risk for these dire health consequences are the same people who often turn to emergency rooms for care and treatment. According to *Oral Health in America: A Report of the Surgeon General* released in 2000, poor adults of all ethnic groups have higher rates of untreated decayed teeth than non-poor adults. African Americans, Latinos, and Native Americans are among the ethnic groups that seem to bear a disproportionate share of the long-term effects of poor oral health care in the United States. As in other areas of health advancement, the substantial gains made in dental science are not evenly distributed across the population. At present, ability to pay for care is the chief determinant of oral health and well-being.

A Fragile Oral Health Safety Net

Community health centers, dental school clinics, hospitals and health departments, and the public health service make up the oral health care safety net for low-income people in the United States. But the resources of these systems are woefully inadequate to meet existing needs and not evenly distributed across populations. Until recently, not all community health centers offered oral health care services, and those that did had difficulty attracting dentists to work in them. In fact, most dentists practice in private offices – businesses with equipment to purchase and bills to pay. Medicaid reimbursement rates for dental care are not comparable to private pay rates; only a small percentage of dentists file Medicaid claims in a given year. And, although Medicaid routinely covers emergency care, many state plans do not reimburse for preventive and restorative dental care. Nationwide Medicaid expenditures for dental care services represent a tiny fraction of payments made overall – in some years, as little as 1 percent.

At the community level, the lack of affordable, accessible dental care creates startling disparities. In remote rural communities and urban areas, the needs of people often exceed the availability of dental facilities and professionals. For dental safety net providers, the relentless demand makes it difficult to focus on prevention. Meeting immediate needs and addressing dental emergencies with the limited resources available are often the only practical options. And the downward spiral of oral health problems is a hard one to interrupt. Untreated cavities in children often lead to gum disease in adulthood. People lose teeth in their prime. Pain and illness cause lost work time and disfigurement, complicate existing health problems (such as diabetes), and often contribute to the development of life-threatening conditions (heart disease, stroke) that lead to premature death. For the underserved and their dental providers, oral health is an unequivocal component of well-being.

Community Voices: Putting Oral Health on the Table

The conceptual framework and design of Community Voices has furnished opportunities to raise access to dental care and oral health as community issues. The initiative's broad definition of health encompasses oral health as an essential element in community well-being. And its approach – to use the community's needs as a starting point rather than existing delivery system capacity – has provided another entrée. By raising oral health as an issue, placing emphasis on addressing community access to dental care, and investing resources accordingly, the Community Voices initiative is clarifying dimensions of the problem and exploring solutions.

Serving as learning laboratories, Community Voices projects are defining the scope of issues inherent in improving access to dental care services for underserved groups. By identifying oral health as a community health issue, Community Voices projects have been able to make progress toward expanding care and informing policy and practice discussions. Collectively, their experiences are contributing to a wider understanding of oral health barriers that cluster around philosophical and perceptual issues, needed data, practice and regulatory parameters, and building the pipeline to produce community-oriented dental health professionals.

Getting Past *"We don't do dental..."*

Community Voices program leaders say this statement sums up the medical provider response to oral health issues. Dental issues are the province of dental science. Care and treatment for the rest of the body is the purview of medical science. Viewed from this perspective, the responsibility of medical safety net providers to address oral health issues is limited. "Oral health is not on the radar screen," as one Community Voices director explains. But community people see things quite differently. And for many Community Voices projects, creating a forum for airing diverse perspectives has prompted some positive action.

Doak Bloss of the Ingham County Community Voices project believes dismissing oral health disparities as "something we can't do anything about" is all too common. But he also believes

Ingham County's experience with oral health is an excellent example of how the Community Voices process rallies stakeholders around an issue. "Saying 'we can't do anything about that' is unacceptable," Bloss states. "Community Voices has been able to demonstrate that such a statement is not true. If you put energy behind an issue, if you put an issue on the table and push it, things happen."

Through a Community Voices "Access to Health" planning and community consensus-building process over a two-year period, stakeholders in Ingham County developed an action plan to create an organized system of care. Increased access to oral health services for community residents is a key strategy in the plan. The plan sets concrete objectives for increasing new mechanisms to streamline and fund access to oral health care and expand the number of dental providers to meet local needs. An Oral Health Task Force is responsible for marshaling resources and support to pursue action plan objectives.

Bloss says the clear direction the plan provides and the widespread agreement it reflects has made it possible to move swiftly as opportunities arise. "Recognizing the lack of oral health services for uninsured and low-income people in our county, the Task Force began working on a proposal for a substantial grant from the state of Michigan to create a dental clinic," he recalls. "With a deadline less than three weeks away, Task Force members gained the cooperation of both local hospitals – each offering space to house a new clinic."

When the grant was awarded, the Healthy Smiles Clinic was built on a site provided by Ingham Regional Medical Center and opened its doors in February 2001. With the addition of the new clinic, by the end of the year almost 6,800 adults and children in Ingham County received services – "people who otherwise would not have been able to access dental care," Bloss emphasizes. The Ingham Health Plan Corporation, the entity governing a health coverage program in the county, has committed $200,000 to expand dental access for uninsured and low-income residents. These and other concerted efforts are raising community and policymaker awareness of the importance of oral health. "Raising awareness is critical," says Bloss, "since many people seem to believe that dental care is a luxury rather than a basic necessity."

"Focusing a Spotlight"

Raising awareness of oral health as an essential part of community well-being is part of the process at work in Community Voices Miami as well. Through a series of community forums held in and around Miami, uninsured and low-income community members talked openly about financial and other barriers to care, including dental services. Their videotaped remarks combined with an oral health study supported by Community Voices is paving the way for some collaboration around increasing access to much-needed dental services.

Leda Perez, director of Community Voices Miami, explains: "In our work around oral health, our project team undertook research to examine what dental services are available to the uninsured and underserved in Miami-Dade. The report showed the dearth of services and the immense need in our county. Perhaps most importantly, the report provided the proof for Camillus Health Concern, a health clinic for the homeless, to justify a grant from the Bureau of Primary Health Care. The grant has allowed Camillus Health Concern to provide dental health services three days a week to the homeless when previously there were none. Recently, a fourth day was added to the service through the assistance of volunteers from the University of Florida."

> *"I'm always surprised by the power of focusing a spotlight on an issue."*
>
> —Jessica Perlmutter, Miami

Perez acknowledges that such services are a small, if important, beginning. And admittedly, raising awareness can only go so far when resources are in short supply. Florida's 2002-2003 fiscal year will likely result in significant cuts to health and human services funds that will only make the challenge greater. Yet this approach nets some gains even in the face of budget cutbacks. Jessica Perlmutter, an active collaborator with Community Voices in her administrative capacity at United Way of Miami-Dade, remarks on its impact and potential. "I'm always surprised by the power of focusing a spotlight on an issue," she says. "It's illuminating. We can see a path more clearly now." The Miami Action Plan for Access to Health Care is a formal document that summarizes the path Perlmutter, Perez, and other Community Voices participants envision. One key objective outlines action steps to increase local dental services capacity and connect oral health to other systems of care.

"The Timing is Now"

Elizabeth Whitley, director of Denver Health Community Voices, believes that the project's efforts to raise awareness about oral health needs and related issues are beginning to gain momentum in Colorado. "It has taken us a long time," she says. "We were the last state to have dental benefits with our Children's Health Insurance Program," she says. "But for us, the timing is now." Denver Health Community Voices' focus on the community's need for expanded dental care services is leveraging additional resources from the Bureau of Primary Health Care, the Caring for Colorado Foundation, and the city and county of Denver. Overall, the expansion will put in place five new dental operatories at two clinics and provide for the purchase of three portable dental chairs and a mobile unit. "The expansions require additional dentists, dental residents, dental hygienists, and assistants," Whitley acknowledges. "But when the new facilities are up and running, they will have the potential to increase dental capacity by 18,400 visits a year."

In Colorado, dental hygienists now can receive reimbursement for services.

To expand long-term oral health services capacity in Colorado, Denver Health Community Voices and its partners are informing state-level discussions about dental provider issues. In Colorado, dental hygienists now can receive reimbursement for services, and dentists working in underserved areas are eligible for loan repayment. The Caring for Colorado Foundation has launched a five-year, $5 million initiative to expand access to dental services in the state by attracting more dentists to practice there. Denver Health Community Voices also is investing in better connections between primary care and oral health services delivery venues to streamline access at the same time. In 2000, internists, family practice, and other primary care practitioners received training to conduct oral health screening at Denver Health clinics. In follow-up surveys, many physicians indicated the program was "a good reminder" to examine patients with oral health issues in mind and refer to dentists as needed.

An Integral Part of Comprehensive Care

Oakland Community Voices' focus on creating comprehensive, integrated coverage and services for Alameda County's low-income residents ensured that dental care would be part of Alliance Family Care, the Alameda County health care coverage product. "Oral health is one of the things that draws families to the program," says Community Voices Director Tomiko Connor. "Dental benefits are an integral part of comprehensive services and a priority in all future product development." Family Care enrollees receive preventative and restorative dental services as part of the overall insurance package through Delta Dental, the California organization providing coverage to state Medicaid and Children's Health Insurance Program participants.

Low-cost dental coverage as part of Alliance Family Care's comprehensive health care is one component of a larger strategy to expand access to oral health care for Alameda County Access to Care Collaborative. Connor explains: "The strategy includes a county plan to conduct oral health screening through the schools and pay for care for those children without access." The Access to Care Collaborative is using what they learn "on the ground" to inform policy discussions as well. Sealants, not originally part of reimbursable services through state coverage plans, were later added based on information shared by Collaborative members – information gleaned as a result of providing dental care to low-income families. Expanded dental care within clinics is another element of the Access to Care Collaborative's strategic direction. La Clinica de La Raza currently offers oral health care services. To add to available options for Family Care enrollees, Asian Health Services is conducting a capital campaign to establish a dental clinic as well.

Data and Analysis to Support Solutions

How big a problem is oral health in underserved communities? What would it take to address unmet needs? How much would it cost, how many practitioners, what types of facilities, and where? These types of questions surface in any practical discussion about providing oral health care for the underserved. In the absence of hard data about the extent of the problem, providers – especially safety net providers who must function with very slim margins and few reserves – are wary about wading into a pond of unmarked depth.

Community Voices projects have come up against this barrier in their attempts to raise oral health issues in their communities. Often, Community Voices efforts highlight the need for credible data to clarify the extent of unmet needs and analysis to counter provider reticence, inform health system decision making, and attract new resources. In some instances, lack of data has a galvanizing effect and ferments active collaboration to answer questions. In other settings, the absence of useful information highlights the need for practice and policy changes in health systems. "El Paso has fewer dentists per capita than most other communities," says Community Voices Director Mary Helen Mays. A predictable condition, according to Pete Duarte, who adds: "We have no dental school, no dental hygienist program. The problem of access to dental care is related to the shortage of providers, and we are a dental health shortage area." Local providers know that many who cannot find care in the United States head south for Juárez, Mexico. But understanding exactly how many people need care is part of the problem, according to Mays. "There was no data on dental care usage in Texas," she explains. "We have had to use data from similar states to frame the issue."

Information to Build an Oral Health Infrastructure
Data and the need for regular assessment has become the focus of the Community Voices Collaborative of the District of Columbia's Oral Health Committee. Judith Johnson, of the D.C. Community Voices Collaborative, says the Committee is part of a needed "oral health infrastructure" to meet the needs of District residents. Dentists, community members, primary care providers, safety net providers, and District of Columbia Department of Health staff come together on the Oral Health Committee. "Plans are underway to conduct an oral health assessment in spring of 2002," she notes. "The assessment is an initial step in the development of a comprehensive oral health plan. It will provide information about existing health system services, resources, providers, specialties, and the needs of residents." Howard University School of Dentistry is the site of a planned summit in late 2002 to release assessment results and strengthen support for establishing an oral health bureau in the District.

Johnson believes Community Voices' role in providing the necessary "legwork" is expediting the work of the Task Force. "There are few dental standards in place that are locally-driven or mandated," she explains. "Research and fact finding are a necessary part of the process to move our work to the next level."

The Voices of Detroit Initiative's (VODI) Oral Health Coalition is building on the need for data collection and strategic planning to expand dental services capacity for Detroit residents. But VODI's Lucille Smith acknowledges, "There are no reliable estimates for lack of dental coverage and few estimates on the level of need." Yet the act of identifying oral health as a core service for VODI members is helping determine the scope of the issue and fuel the expansion of services. Local providers, the city of Detroit, and the Delta Dental insurance company are among the collaborating organizations actively involved in building an infrastructure for delivering dental care services to Detroit's underserved. Already, through Community Voices efforts and with support from the city of Detroit, a new adult dental care clinic with three dental chairs is serving 60 patients a week. In addition, service capacity at another local clinic has been expanded by two chairs.

VODI has developed an oral health education module for primary care providers.

Although these measures represent improved oral health care capacity in Detroit, VODI's partner organizations are collaborating with institutions of higher learning to expand access to dental care and needed data beyond current limits. VODI has developed an oral health education module for primary care providers. Created and disseminated in CD form, the content provides training on how to screen for oral health problems. Both Wayne State University and the University of Michigan are offering continuing education credits for physicians and other providers who complete the curriculum. In affiliation with the University of Michigan Dental School, VODI also is participating in the establishment of a Center for Oral Health Disparities. The Center's research objectives will provide valuable data for VODI partners, academic institutions, and community leaders – information about existing disparities in Detroit's poorest African-American communities and indicators for improving oral health.

Identifying Practice and Regulatory Barriers

As Community Voices participants move to increase access to oral health care in their communities, they must first sort through the array of policies that guide the provision of dental services in their states. As they do, they encounter practice and regulatory parameters – licensure, reimbursement, and related issues – that can hinder and even obstruct the development of cost-effective, practical solutions to expanding oral health services. As they identify barriers, raise awareness about the extent of community need, and build on coalitions of stakeholders, Community Voices participants are sharing what they learn with public and institutional policymakers.

A Strong Coalition to Address Systemic Issues

The West Virginia Community Voices Partnership began putting some serious effort into oral health issues as part of the West Virginia Welfare Reform Coalition. The Coalition was asked to develop specific recommendations about oral health services for Temporary Assistance for Needy Families (TANF) recipients and developed guidelines that would provide people moving from welfare to work with dental care as part of the state's overall support for their transition. They reasoned that people who hoped to become employable needed a way to address oral health issues as part of their general health. "The initial reaction to the recommendations was lukewarm," Nancy Tolliver of West Virginia Community Voices admits. "But since that time, most of the recommendations have been developed by the West Virginia Department of Health and Human Resources. Eight million dollars in TANF funds was dedicated. Medicaid dental care reimbursement for providers was increased to more adequately pay for both adult and child oral health services. And the change is expected to increase the availability of dental providers willing to serve Medicaid and TANF recipients."

Building on the impact of Coalition work, West Virginia Community Voices formed an Oral Health Task Force to raise awareness on oral health issues and provide a focal point for collaboration. The strategy is working, Tolliver believes. "The Task

Force has developed a repository of data about oral health status, supply, and demand in West Virginia and is providing leadership to keep the focus on this issue," she says. The Oral Health Task Force was invited to represent West Virginia at a National Governors Association meeting on oral health – making it possible for Task Force members to work side-by-side with the state Dental Health Association decision makers, state policymakers, the Bureau of Public Health, and West Virginia University Dental School. Relationships brokered at that meeting are helping the Task Force unite a stronger coalition and, over time, intensify the spotlight on oral health issues in the state. "The Oral Health Policy Task Force is a wonderful example of how Community Voices was the catalyst in bringing key partners to the table and organizing a group that has become a dynamic force on its own," states Tolliver. In the 2002 legislative session, Tolliver reports that the Oral Health Task Force provided background that informed the development of state-level oral health priorities and resulted in the creation of an Office of Oral Health in the Department of Health and Human Resources.

The ripple effect of drawing attention to oral health issues and fostering collaboration to address them is already being felt at the community level. For example, the state public health bureau committed funding to provide partial support for expanded dental services at a community clinic in Charleston. The center has three new dental chairs and increased capacity to provide oral health care to Charleston's most vulnerable. Collaboration with the West Virginia University School of Dentistry also is producing new information on how to teach parents of very young children the importance of oral health. A pilot program based on this study will bring new education approaches to rural health centers in the state.

Connecting Clinical Capacity to Practice and Policy
In North Carolina, FirstHealth Community Voices is expanding dental services to children of low-income families at three centers in three different counties and targeting future expansion to reach adults. "But when we first started," remembers Lisa Hartsock of FirstHealth Community Voices, "there seemed to be so many barriers to address." Some barriers related to financing and the extent of the need. As Hartsock explains: "Dental care was the number

one unmet need for low-income children in the region. An estimated 12,000 children were medically underserved with no dental coverage and no access to dental care." That obstacle seemed formidable, but there were others – provider shortages, local capacity, and provider perceptions among them.

Despite the obvious gap in services, FirstHealth was somewhat hesitant about moving into oral health. "We perceived that local dentists were not sure they wanted FirstHealth to provide dental services," says Hartsock. But data from FirstHealth providers and state public health agencies made the case for the unmet need, and a task force that included local dental providers confirmed that the demand for services exceeded the capacity of existing providers to address on their own. "North Carolina only has 38 dentists for every 100,000 people," Hartsock notes. "The national average is 60 per 100,000." The next step was determining the scope of services, identifying resources, and finding and hiring community-oriented providers. "Local dentists, human services personnel, and community members came together to discuss the program's purpose and eligibility requirements," says Hartsock. Sharon Nicolson Harrell, D.D.S., M.P.H., was hired as dental director of the FirstHealth program. Hartsock believes Dr. Harrell's leadership has been instrumental in addressing remaining issues as the program has evolved.

"Dental care was the number one unmet need for low-income children in the region."

—Lisa Hartsock,
North Carolina

Today, three FirstHealth dental clinics operating in Hoke, Montgomery, and Moore counties serve more than 7,000 children – close to 60 percent of the underserved target population. In the process of staffing the clinics and evaluating the overall cost of operations, FirstHealth Community Voices is learning about how to provide dental care services to meet the needs of this population. Offering dental services has proven to be a way to reach medically underserved families and link them with existing programs. "Clinic staff determined that many of the children's families would qualify for public assistance, so they implemented a policy of routinely assisting client families with the application process for available programs," Hartsock says. "Initially, this helped convert uninsured to 'insured' at a rate of 1 percent a month!"

Currently 88 percent of children seen at the clinics are covered by some public health program – CHIP or Medicaid. Dental services require a small co-payment and connect participants with FirstHealth transportation services to reduce the likelihood of missed appointments. Staff members with bilingual skills are recruited to overcome language barriers for Spanish-speaking clients. By taking both consumer and provider issues seriously, Hartsock believes FirstHealth is making progress on a number of fronts. "FirstHealth dental clinics have a 'no-show' rate of half the American Dental Association rate," she offers as one indicator of the utility of this approach. "Although the clinics are not expected to break even, they are maintained with FirstHealth's Community Benefit investment equal to 10 percent of the program's annual operating budget," she adds.

Trying to find ways to use existing resources to improve the oral health of children connects the clinical work at FirstHealth dental clinics with state-level reimbursement and practice issues. As Dr. Harrell explains: "Providing care to underserved children gives us a unique perspective that is critical in raising state-level discussions on practice and policy issues. My colleagues and I are aware of barriers to care which can then be communicated to leaders at the state level." Harrell serves on the North Carolina Institute of Medicine Task Force on Dental Care Access, a group that has been instrumental in raising policymaker and public awareness about oral health issues. For instance, dental sealants, a low-cost way to protect children's teeth from tooth decay that Harrell calls "one of the cornerstones of preventive services," were not originally part of North Carolina's CHIP benefits. "The Task Force, along with the North Carolina Oral Health Section, the North Carolina Academy of Pediatric Dentistry, and other agencies, expressed their concern about the program's viability in light of the limited scope of services," she recalls. Since then, sealants have become part of the state's CHIP package.

Fluoride varnish is another cost-effective way to prevent tooth decay in infants and very young children. In North Carolina, state regulations traditionally limited reimbursement for that procedure to dentists in conjunction with a dental cleaning. Yet infants and children under the age of 3 are far more likely to see a pediatrician in the first years of life. To make it possible for pediatricians and other primary care providers to administer fluoride varnish, conduct oral health screenings, and receive Medicaid reimbursement for these services, Dr. Harrell helped bring a preventive fluoride dental care program, "Into the Mouths of Babes," to the area and organized a training session for local physicians, physician's assistants, nurse practitioners, and other pediatric medical professionals. Already, more than 160 physicians, nurses, and staff have completed the training. Dr. Harrell and her colleagues see other opportunities to inform practice and regulatory policies to expand oral health access for underserved people. For example, during Dr. Harrell's tenure as a legislative dentist with the North Carolina Dental Society, she helped to address the issue of licensure-by-credentials which would make it easier for dentists licensed in other states to consider practicing in North Carolina.

Hartsock credits Community Voices as the impetus for FirstHealth's broad view of oral health issues. "Because of the tremendous need, FirstHealth would have pursued providing clinic services even without Community Voices, but I am not sure the program would have gone beyond providing direct services," says Hartsock. "The Community Voices orientation challenges us to think bigger. While many dental providers might be focused on day-to-day operations, Community Voices has challenged us to engage others in addressing policy and practice barriers. The initiative has also enabled us to better share our local strategies with other communities as we strive to improve oral health."

Wanted: Community-Oriented Dental Providers

Community Voices program participants know that the shortage of community-oriented dental providers limits their overall capacity to expand oral health services. As one Community Voices leader put it, "Providers aren't exactly standing in line to work on low-income people." Shortages now are one issue Community Voices confronts as it attempts to piece together expanded care options for underserved populations. But it recognizes that "pipeline issues" are another dimension of the problem.

A Shrinking Pipeline Complicates Expanding Oral Health

A large proportion of underserved people are people of color – African Americans, Latinos, American Indians, and immigrants. In the next few decades, Census Bureau figures project that people in these groups will make up an even larger portion of the general population. Yet the number of minority students in dental programs nationwide has been shrinking in recent years. Jeanne Sinkford, D.D.S., and director of the Division of Equity and Diversity at the American Dental Education Association, sees a clear connection between the decline in minority enrollment in dental schools and limited oral health access for the underserved. "We believe significant underrepresentation translates into the lack of availability of services in minority communities," she states.

In the 1980s, a number of dental schools closed leaving the total figure at 54 dental schools in 32 states. Nationally, enrollment in dental schools is down in general, but declining enrollment among minority students is particularly worrisome. Practice patterns indicate that minority dentists are more likely to provide services in minority communities. Dental educators speculate that the cost of dental education may be a factor in enrollment and the likelihood of graduates to practice in underserved areas. Most dental students assume $100,000 in debt even before they undertake advanced training. With financial obligations on that scale, few young dentists of any ethnicity can afford to begin practicing in low-income communities.

Nationally, enrollment in dental schools is down ... but declining enrollment among minority students is particularly worrisome.

To address these existing disparities and begin to build the pipeline of community-oriented dental providers, several Community Voices projects are making a concerted effort to partner with academic institutions. In addition to the efforts in progress through the Voices of Detroit Initiative, FirstHealth Dental Care Centers are functioning as a rotation site for University of North Carolina dental students and Fayetteville Technical Community College dental hygiene and dental assistant students. Other North Carolina collaborations are in the works with Sandhills Community College to develop dental hygiene and assistant programs, as well as the development of a mentoring program for high school students. In Baltimore, Vision for Health Community Voices is working with the University of Maryland Dental School to offer a community rotation for dental students at neighborhood clinics. And in El Paso, Community Voices is exploring a partnership with Baylor University to expand dental care to the uninsured. Dental students in El Paso also may receive a housing stipend to help defray educational costs. These and other connections newly formed are linking the needs of underserved communities with health professions education decision making – connections with the potential to shape practice parameters over time.

Taking the Lead in Dental Education and Community-Focused Service Delivery

As the lead partner for Northern Manhattan Community Voices, Columbia University's School of Dental and Oral Surgery is also the primary dental care provider for underserved people in the Central Harlem and Washington Heights neighborhoods. In recognition of this role, Dean Allan J. Formicola, D.D.S., and his colleagues on the Columbia faculty determined it was necessary to inter-relate dental education with community-focused services to reduce barriers to oral health care. In 1994, the school formed the Community DentCare Network, a partnership with the Harlem Hospital Dental Service and local providers, schools, churches, and community organizations. In addition to full-service dental care at neighborhood sites, Community DentCare provides preventative services – education, screening, dental cleaning, and sealants – at six school-based clinics. "Ultimately," Dr. Formicola and his colleagues wrote a few years after the formation of DentCare, "dental schools must educate students in an environment that places emphasis on the needs of the entire public – both the economically disadvantaged and those who can afford to pay for care – and, at the same time, stimulate some graduates to enter into research and public service careers."

With the benefit of leadership on this scale, Northern Manhattan Community Voices is building upon Network activities and resources to expand oral health care services to underserved community members. The project's Difficult-to-Cover Services Working Group is the focal point for oral health issues, according to Northern Manhattan Community Voices Executive Director Sandra Harris. "The Working Group has a dual mandate to enhance access to both mental and dental health services," she explains. In 2001, the Group's efforts resulted in "a remarkable surge" in activities related to oral health. The release of Surgeon General David Satcher's report on the "silent epidemic" of oral health disease helped put the issue "on the policy radar screen," Harris says. At an American Public Health Association meeting, Dr. Satcher and New York State Department of Health Commissioner Dr. Antonia Novello participated in a forum on the issue. "This momentum was vital," Harris believes – and has played an important role in implementing additional dental services locally.

The opening of the Mannie L. Wilson Senior Medical and Dental Center in Harlem is one clear outcome of the community focus on oral health issues. In community meetings, elderly residents repeatedly pointed to their need for dental care. "Seniors said, 'It's nice that kids have services, but we need them too,'" Harris recalls. Located on the site of a public hospital closed under community protest, the Center now houses medical offices and seven dental operatories. And in East Harlem, dental services are available at the Boriken Community Health Center as well. Community Voices partnerships also made it possible to add a seventh school-based clinic to the Community DentCare Network sites.

"Seniors said, 'It's nice that kids have services, but we need them too.'"

—*Sandra Harris, New York*

Through the efforts of Northern Manhattan Community Voices, a productive collaboration with Children's Aid Society is making dental care available at day care centers and Head Start sites. A state-of-the-art oral health care facility on wheels, DentCare's Mobile Dental Van is equipped with x-ray, two dental chairs, and space for one-on-one patient instruction. In addition to visiting schools and other sites targeting children, the van is making the rounds at senior centers and health fairs. In the last six months of 2001, the new facility provided services to more than 1,300 underserved children and adults. Overall, the Community DentCare Network and its partnerships provided 28,000 patient visits in 2001.

To strengthen the pipeline of dental professionals from their communities, Northern Manhattan Community Voices contributed to the development of a dental assistant training program. The one-year program has graduated its second class of dental assistants, most, residents of the neighborhoods around Columbia

University. Harris emphasizes the link between this program and the overall thrust of Community Voices. "The dental assistant program addresses two of the collaborative's main objectives – increasing the number of minority providers in the oral health field and workforce development. Because the program identifies community residents and equips them with the necessary skills to enter the oral health field," she says, "many of the students who have gone through the program are currently working in their natural communities."

Community-Driven Oral Health Links Programs, Education, and Practice

Although the University of New Mexico (UNM) was a primary provider of health care services for the underserved at the outset of Community Voices, the lead partner's chief connection with oral health issues prior to the initiative was through its dental hygiene program and related services. Yet since the inception of Community Voices Shared Solutions, UNM has taken the lead in expanding access to dental care for underserved residents, creating new opportunities to address provider shortages through education and informing state-level policies that impact practice issues. Wayne Powell, associate director of the Center for Community Partnerships at UNM, says, "Oral health options and policies have been dramatically influenced by the University's new role as educator and provider of services."

The providers who are practicing in New Mexico are more likely to be working in cities than across the state's wide rural expanses.

The need for expanded oral health care in New Mexico is indisputable. New Mexico has no dental school, and the state ranks 49th of 50 in its dentist-to-population ratio. Twenty-eight of 33 counties are recognized as dental health provider shortage areas. The providers who are practicing in New Mexico are more likely to be working in cities than across the state's wide rural expanses. And the mean age of practicing dentists in the state is 50, suggesting that without intervention, matters could only go from bad to worse.

Powell says Shared Solutions set oral health objectives for program efforts. "We wanted to increase access to address unmet need, but also to restore the public health perspective in oral health. To do that, we knew we needed to increase interdisciplinary capacity and develop responsive policies for financing, best practices, and education," he explains. "Our overall approach was to work from the community as the basis for change."

Following the sponsorship of a statewide oral health summit to raise awareness and gather possible stakeholders, Shared Solutions formed the New Mexico Oral Health Council to bring together private providers, state agencies, Indian Health Service administrators, federal programs, community advocates, other regional educational institutions, and professional organizations. At the community level, Shared Solutions was deepening connections with rural groups to better understand their interests, existing resources, and the scope of unmet needs. When Stephen Beetstra, D.D.S., was hired as dental services director, Shared Solutions' Oral Health Initiative was off and running.

Beetstra reports he is now one of nine full-time dentists rotating through an equal number of community dental sites in New Mexico. All are on faculty at UNM and provide direct services as well as oversee emergency and family practice medical students from UNM and dental students from the University of North Carolina who rotate through the clinics. Some facilities are operated by the University of New Mexico; others are dental facilities at outreach clinics or federally qualified health centers. The UNM dentists and staff dental hygienists drive or fly to reach the nine sites and provide services to people who would otherwise have no access to care.

UNM dental programs are funded through a patchwork of financing involving a wide range of collaborators and public programs geared to address indigent health, and they are filling a tremendous need, Beetstra notes. "In Lordsburg (one rural clinic site), they had not had a dentist there for 45 years," he offers. "At another clinic site, developmentally disabled people had to travel five hours just to receive services." But Beetstra says UNM's dental services division is changing that scenario. In one year, the dentists and hygienists from the UNM Division of Dental Services provided care to more than 23,600 adults and children at outreach clinics, federally qualified health centers, and university-operated sites.

"I take my turn just like everyone else," Dr. Beetstra says cheerfully. Talking during a lunch break from his day in one of the clinics, he was working on the program's budget during the noon hour as well. Beetstra says all the dentists in the program are engaged in every aspect of expanded access to oral health – from providing services to sharing what they know about dental health and practice issues to inform policy discussions.

The level of community involvement is crucial to expanding services, according to Beetstra, and the Roswell clinic in Chavez County is one telling example of how important community direction can be. "Roswell started as a grassroots effort to get dental services for local underserved kids," Beetstra says. Wayne Powell agrees and adds, "Steve Gonzales, a Roswell plumber and community activist, got involved when a local health center used county funds to purchase a mobile dental van and then failed to implement services. Steve went and got the van, the community repaired it, and they began working with Eastern New Mexico University-Roswell Branch to get pro-bono services from local dentists to staff it. We were making trips to Roswell and having discussions about oral health at the same time and became involved." Working with the Department of Health, Eastern New Mexico University, the city of Roswell, and other stakeholders, Shared Solutions collaboration made expanded oral health services in Roswell a reality.

> "Roswell started as a grassroots effort to get dental services for local underserved kids."
> —Stephen Beetstra, New Mexico

Beetstra and Powell underscore that adding services in Roswell is only part of the story. As Powell explains: "Eastern New Mexico University had already planned to initiate a dental assistant program in Roswell. To contribute to that effort, our discussions have been around faculty support, our dentists providing educational experiences and training sites, and the possibilities that some dental assistant graduates may want to enter the UNM Dental Hygienist program. We also envisioned the placement of dental assistants from the community in local practices." Beetstra echoes that sentiment and says that dental assistants from the community *are* finding local employment, noting one particularly fitting placement: "Steve's daughter, Sabrina, graduated from the program and was hired at the Roswell clinic!"

On Fridays, Beetstra says that staff try to get together to discuss state-level issues that impact their ability to provide needed services. Working closely with the Oral Health Council, Beetstra and his colleagues – some of whom have experience in state agencies and the Indian Health Service – pool what they know firsthand about the needs of underserved people in New Mexico and practices that could improve access to oral health care. In response to information provided through the Oral Health Council and community needs, New Mexico has acted to raise the Medicaid dental reimbursement, create a state Division of Dental Services within the state Medicaid office, make changes in state regulation to allow dental hygienists to practice independently, allocate funding to train dentists to serve developmentally disabled people, and expand the New Mexico Health Service Corps to include dentists and dental hygienists.

Many New Mexico residents are still without access to oral health services, Powell admits. But connections relating programs to expand services with education to build a pipeline of providers – and then with state-level discussions that shape the practice and regulatory environment – are beginning to improve access for underserved people.

Chapter 5:
Broad Community Interests Reorient Approaches to Building a Stronger Safety Net

- *"The only way to solve community problems – or to engage in creative and strategic thinking that leads to solutions – is by engaging the people who are directly affected in the process. This is the Community Voices approach. Local folks identify strategies and promising practices that may never occur to people outside of the immediate 'community of common purpose.' By providing local communities with meaningful information and linking them to outside resources, local initiative is supported and community self-interest catalyzed."* –Steve Heasley, financing and program consultant, West Virginia Governor's Cabinet on Children and Families

- *"Public policymakers worry about expanding coverage for uninsured and underserved. They say, 'It will require too much investment. They'll be too sick. They'll use too many services. They won't pay for coverage.' But our focus groups indicated that low-income people were not so different from everybody else. People in the community told us, 'If we find value and it's affordable, we'll buy it.' And as it turns out, they were right. The people who have enrolled in Family Care are not generally in poor health, they don't misuse services, and they pay premiums."* –Irene Ibarra, CEO, Alameda Alliance for Health, California

- *"All the signs indicated that market-based health care policies would reduce the capacity to provide services to low-income, uninsured people. But instead of losing ground, this community created an organization that now has a budget and a set of coverage programs sufficient to help about 85 percent of the low-income uninsured in the county. The value of the Community Voices approach is that solutions are found that could not be found before."* –Marcus Cheatham, health analyst, Ingham County, Michigan

- *"This approach brings many relevant voices together around common issues. This creates an enhanced sense of trust among stakeholders and builds the group's strength as a coalition."* –Mary Stephens Ferris, president and CEO, Detroit Community Health Connection, Inc.

Each and every one of the Community Voices projects has its testimonials – heartfelt endorsements like these from "believers" who have seen the power of community interests in action. Perhaps that's because, within each project, the real-life community voices are many and varied – underserved consumers of health care services, providers, decision makers from public and community institutions, elected officials, business people, religious leaders, and more. At the community level, all have faces and names and perspectives about health issues and what to do about them. For that reason, Community Voices participants emphasize, *all* have a role in the process. All are stakeholders with an enduring and necessary interest in the viability of the community safety net. And all need to be heard.

Yet members of each group – employers, providers, consumers, public agencies – often work to find solutions to common problems in relative isolation. And all too often, the people most vitally affected by changes in safety net systems have little opportunity to share what they know with those working in institutions and organizations – to raise issues, educate decision makers, and craft programmatic solutions. Community Voices project leaders and participants believe that attention to process is crucial to developing workable products. By creating mechanisms to learn from and engage *all* stakeholders, Community Voices projects are harnessing both the passion and pragmatism of broad community interests and reorienting approaches to building a stronger safety net.

"Don't Tell Me 'No,' Tell Me How!"

Statements like this one – emphatic, impatient, and refreshingly to the point – have been uttered at one time or another in every Community Voices project. The people most often making the statement are close enough to community issues to understand how lack of access to health care services and related challenges tinge everyday life. Community interests create urgency, project leaders have learned. They can "light a fire" under entrenched interests and make it difficult or impossible to ignore community needs in the face of customary obstacles. People in health systems, public agencies, and other institutions acknowledge that the kind of resolve the Community Voices process engenders can be a mighty force. But they also recognize that initiating a respectful conversation between the underserved and institutional and other decision makers is a delicate dance requiring care, tact, and a broad view of community. As one participant advises, "Know your community at multiple levels – politically, economically, culturally, and by neighborhood."

"We promote citizen engagement..."
The West Virginia Community Voices Partnership took up this challenge in 1999 by sponsoring a dozen community forums on health care. Sponsored in partnership with local and state coalitions, the sessions offered a venue for thoughtful discussion about health, coverage, and access to care. *Filling West Virginia's Health Care Cracks: What Should We Do About Uninsured Children and Families?* was a video and discussion guide developed to spark public deliberation. More than 200 participants considered the complexities of expanding health care access and coverage, but also voiced their interests and desires. To continue the conversation and widen the circle of interest, the West Virginia Community Voices Partnership summarized key themes from the forums into a briefing paper for institutional and state policymakers.

> *"By modeling public discourse on complex issues, we promote citizen engagement."*
>
> —Renate Pore,
> West Virginia

Building on these first forums, West Virginia Community Voices partners undertook a second series of public gatherings in 2000. "Making Ends Meet: What Should We Do About Working Families?" was a discussion platform for 35 community meetings across the state. Renate Pore, a past director of the West Virginia Community Voices project who continues to be active in her role as director of the Governor's Cabinet on Children and Families, explains the overall process and how it expands engagement and dialogue: "Following each set of forums, we would summarize findings, publish them, and deliver these to decision makers. By modeling public discourse on complex issues, we promote citizen engagement. We show poor, rural, minority, and other underserved West Virginians that they have a voice and that it counts."

At the heart of this approach, Pore says, is a conviction that the best way of improving the health of people in West Virginia is "by addressing the perplexing determinants of poor health – lack of inclusion, powerlessness, helplessness, and hopelessness." Each Community Voices project has fashioned some version of this cycle of engagement to raise issues and draw stakeholders into a productive dialogue. Although efforts are independent and scattered across the 13 sites, collectively they begin to articulate some important messages about community desires for health and health care.

What Communities Value

In June 2001, the Community Voices initiative published a report that distills themes from a collection of surveys, focus groups, and forums involving nearly 5,000 participants – as well as findings from the 1999 Community Voices national public opinion survey. The final product – a booklet entitled, *What Communities Value About Health and Health Care* – draws on both the connections formed through Community Voices and the experiences of program leaders across sites.

Reflecting on the results of project-level surveys, focus groups, and forums, Community Voices project directors helped frame a series of questions as the springboard for 34 additional focus groups held in six states. The sessions were designed to elicit insights from a broad spectrum of underserved community members nationwide – including urban and rural residents, immigrants, people of color, and low-income workers. Comments made at videotaped sessions served to reiterate important messages and underscore the key messages contained in the summary (available online at www.communityvoices.org). *What Communities Value About Health and Health Care* identifies five key values at the core of many Community Voices efforts:

- *Trust and respect* – the need to focus on relationships, continuity, and cultural competency in health services delivery;

- *Care for the "whole person"* – services and systems that encompass, as one man put it, "the mental, the physical, the emotional, the spiritual";

- *Care when and where people need it* – attention to how and where services are provided to draw people into appropriate, needed care;

• *Affordable coverage for everyone* – so no one needs to go "begging to be healthy," as one woman expressed it; and

• *Healthy communities* – recognizing that poverty, housing, transportation, and environmental issues are intrinsically linked to community health.

To respond to community interests – and create a framework for comprehensive approaches to community health – Community Voices projects are establishing structures for ongoing dialogue, placing community interests at the center of programs, and looking beyond health to address the disparities that constrain underserved communities.

Creating Structures for Ongoing Dialogue

Advisory councils, workgroups, and other collaborative boards formed or strengthened by Community Voices help change the balance of power and ensure a voice for underserved community interests.

In some projects, the focus is on broadening participation in existing structures. For instance, the West Virginia Family Resource Networks (FRNs) represent a state strategy for building community capacity. "A state-federal partnership funds 46 FRNs in West Virginia," Renate Pore explains. "Community Voices has invested in strengthening the FRNs in our four-county area to expand community engagement." Part-time associate directors provide staff support to community groups that connect service providers, community leaders, and local residents. West Virginia Community Voices Partnership Project Director Nancy Tolliver says, "The groups work to complete community health assessments, choose and implement projects related to identified needs, link people to services, and support community action to address health status and health access." The community action facilitated through West Virginia FRNs supports change at the local level and becomes a building block for tackling state-level issues as well. FRNs are the "core partner," Tolliver notes, in establishing a statewide collaborative Mental Health Policy Task Force that is identifying barriers to mental health care access and offering recommendations. By linking community experiences with state-level discussions, the Task Force is seeing tangible evidence of the wider impact of this approach. In 2002, the Governor included a mental health parity act in his legislative agenda.

Structures to Amplify Community Voice

In a related strategy, the Community Voices Collaborative of the District of Columbia is strengthening structures for coordinating resources and amplifying community voice in decision making. "The strategy is to build upon access initiatives already in formative stages in the D.C. Department of Health," according to Executive Director Judith Johnson.

> *"The message to men and the people who love them is to seek care before conditions become life threatening."*
>
> —*Judith Johnson, District of Columbia*

The Men's Health Initiative, recently unveiled by the D.C. Department of Health, is incorporating information gathered through Community Voices Collaborative efforts in 2000 – especially a series of focus groups to identify issues related to adolescent and men's health. "The focus groups surfaced three issues for men in general – delivering health services where men are likely to be, the need for services that are not female-oriented, and cost barriers," Johnson recaps. "These results were compiled and used as fodder in meetings with the community, Collaborative partners, and the Department of Health." The first stage of efforts in response to this information is a prevention campaign targeting the District's African-American and Latino men. "The message to men and the people who love them is to seek care before conditions become life threatening," says Johnson. In addition to the public awareness campaign, community health outreach workers are linking these efforts with enrollment in the D.C. HealthCare Alliance coverage program, focusing on men who are not caring for children.

Long term, Community Voices Collaborative participants are targeting the development of a men's health clinic. Ronald E. Lewis, senior deputy director for health promotion in the D.C. Department of Health, states, "A system of care that ensures healthy outcomes for men must be accessible, culturally sensitive, and accountable; have a multidisciplinary focus; and be based on client and service performance data."

A Sustainable Mechanism to Guide Decision Making
Elsewhere, Community Voices groups are establishing new bodies
to articulate community interests within health system infrastruc-
tures. The FirstHealth Community Health Board in North Carolina
is a regional advisory group "on the same level as other FirstHealth
entity boards," says FirstHealth Community Voices Director Lisa
Hartsock. "But it has a different nomination and selection process.
Nominees come from community groups rather than internal recommendations," resulting in important differences in perspective.

Hartsock sees a variety of ways the Community Health Board
is shaping the dialogue inside and outside of FirstHealth. "The
local focus of Board members brings a different light to everything.
They relate local issues to regional decision making. And they find
advocates at the local level, sometimes making it possible to ease a
program or service into the community. They know the people,
the issues, the local concerns." Community Health Board members
also recognize when something will not be well received at the
community level. Hartsock recalls one example. "We started to
talk about a master patient index as a mechanism for sharing data
among providers. When the concept was under discussion, one
Community Health Board member remarked, 'Sounds like "Big
Brother!"' That reminded us that patient concerns about privacy
might not view this approach as a positive thing," she remembers.

Hartsock perceives that the significance of the Community
Health Board lies in its guidance and impact over time. "The Board
is a sustainable mechanism for maintaining community voice and
input into health system decision making," she says. By connecting the interests of diverse communities with service and programmatic decisions within health systems, the Board structure places
community interests in a pivotal position within the health system.

Collaborations Raise a Chorus
Community Voices projects are cutting across traditional silos – of
business, education, health care, neighborhoods, and nonprofits –
to raise common challenges. Collaborations connect interests
across issues making it possible for consumers, business and community leaders, educators, health system decision makers, and
public administrators to think and act together.

Marty Lucia, assistant director of the Dade County Health Policy Authority, has been a participant of Community Voices Miami since its inception and says, "It is essential to get the various factions and future collaborators sitting down and talking about how to creatively solve problems." Generating formal, broad-based collaboration at that level has been Community Voices Miami's focus. "The strength is its framework," he states. "It serves as an all-encompassing 'master facilitator' in trying to bring together various health care entities, many of which do not usually sit at the same table.

"*Community Voices Miami ... serves as an all-encompassing 'master facilitator...'*"

—Marty Lucia, Miami

"Community Voices Miami brings together the highly respected RAND organization for research and technical assistance, and the local United Way of Miami-Dade County as the expert in engaging the local community," he continues.

But the group that combines leadership and consensus-building among health care services stakeholders across the community is the local Multi-Agency Consortium (MAC), formed through Community Voices Miami, Lucia says. "The local framework of the project has the strength of a leadership group which will provide the political and business power to make changes based on the MAC and Oversight Team's goals and objectives under the Miami Action Plan."

Fact-Finding and Groundwork to Engage Stakeholders
To build collaboration and address the reservations of key stakeholders, the California Rural Indian Health Board (CRIHB) draws would-be skeptics into the process of exploring options firsthand. CRIHB's Andy Anderson cites two group trips to Seattle, Washington, to learn about a successful community-owned managed care organization. The fact-finding forays helped deepen understanding about the potential of the Turtle Health Plan model and build support. "Representatives from seven separate Indian Health Programs participated in the visits," Anderson says. "The questions they asked and responses they received were shared with many more through the *Tuesdays with Turtle* newsletter."

Articles in other publications disseminated information gained through the process, helping educate potential stakeholders. In an article published in the *Southern California Physician*, Dr. Tim Nicely, medical director of the United Indian Health Services in Arcata, spoke about the impact of the Washington trips. "I never imagined that I'd have any interest in putting together a health-insurance company," he told a reporter. But that changed when he visited the Seattle community clinics with peers from other Indian Health Programs and became taken with "the idea of setting up a health plan in which the people providing the care and the people who owned the health plan were the same people."

Now a member of the Turtle Health Plan board of directors, Nicely says, "The Turtle Health Plan represents the essence of what managed care should be and was supposed to be – a system which manages the cost of health care services in a context where quality of care and the needs of our patients remain paramount." Anderson attributes the support Turtle has among Indian Health Program medical directors as stemming from this kind of ground-work among key stakeholders. "Doctors need to hear it from other doctors," he believes.

"Speak as one voice . . ."
By exerting leadership to support timely collaboration at the local level, Community Voices El Paso is serving community interests while highlighting pressing issues. In its work with the West Texas CHIP Collaborative, for example, Community Voices El Paso helped meet and exceed enrollment targets for eligible children in the community. Jose Moreno, former Community Voices director who currently is working with the United Neighborhood Organization in El Paso, talks about the significance of this suc-cessful collaborative effort. "The activities really go toward what we are trying to show," he explains. "Local initiatives and local efforts are the key to being successful. We need to collaborate and work as a community."

At an October 2001 Community Voices El Paso symposium on access to quality health care, Moreno says participants under-scored the importance of collaboration. "Facing an $8 billion shortfall in the Texas budget for 2002," Moreno recalls, "we were reminded by several of the speakers that unless we work together and speak as one voice, we would face cuts and not be able to pro-tect what we have achieved for underserved children so far."

Holding Feet to the Fire

Community Voices structures are going beyond raising issues to create mechanisms for accountability – formal agreements that specify expectations and provide a process for pursuing and measuring progress toward goals.

The Voices of Detroit Initiative (VODI) has developed these formal connections to strengthen the coalition and provide a basis for ongoing work. "VODI has written affiliation arrangements for the continuum of care," explains VODI's Lucille Smith. The agreements reflect a form of system collaboration that Smith describes as "hard-nosed and pragmatic." But it is a realistic, business-like approach that establishes stronger connections for VODI's long-term efforts and sets forth partner expectations.

The agreements are making it possible to expand services now and address longstanding health disparities through future collaboration. Smith cites the provision of pharmacy services to Detroit's underserved as a prime example of how these connections are working. "People enrolled in VODI have access to primary care, prescription, and laboratory services as a result of this formal collaboration. The health department and health systems are providing prescription and laboratory services; the clinics provide primary care in Detroit neighborhoods," Smith says. "The agreements between clinics, the city, and health systems make this comprehensive care possible."

VODI is a realistic, business-like approach.

VODI is building on the experience of cooperation at this level to tackle mental health issues next. "Untreated depression, substance abuse, and mental illness are often seen in Detroit's uninsured population," Smith notes. "VODI partners see a high number of behavioral health problems in their emergency departments." Working closely with Detroit's federally qualified health centers, the Community Mental Health Board, the city and county, and local health systems, VODI is tracking mental health needs among Detroit's underserved, and identifying the education needs of providers and the resources required to care for patients.

VODI's long-term goal is an integrated delivery system that provides a continuum of care for Detroit's uninsured and underserved. The "hard-nosed" collaboration among VODI partners is crucial to creating that system, Smith believes. And she sees evidence that institutional structures are changing in ways that will support the development of deeper connections to better serve community interests. "One health system has established a 'director of safety net' position; two systems actually code patients as 'VODI.' We're not where we were five years ago," she admits. "But we are a different group of partners at the table."

Accountable to the Community

In Ingham County, the *Ingham Action Plan for an Organized System of Care* represents a cycle of activity that links stakeholders to accountability for pursuing community interests related to health. More than 300 people from various stakeholder groups offered their insights and analysis over many months to form the Ingham Action Plan. Through a reiterative process – one in which the products of each session were shared across the community to reach new groups; spark dialogue; and refine beliefs, values, and objectives – Ingham County consumers, employers, insurers, and providers developed a common agenda.

The agenda outlines seven broad goals related to health care coverage in Ingham County, access to care, unmet community needs, outreach, and oversight. Stating goals is not a great departure from the work of other such community efforts, but the Ingham Action Plan takes this process a few steps further. Each goal has specific objectives and indicators to make it possible to evaluate progress. And each objective assigns a lead agency charged with the task of coordinating efforts and making sure the work gets done. As the Ingham Action Plan report states: "Although the Access to Healthcare Committee of the Capital Area Health Alliance will remain the coordinating body for the Action Plan, the work to be done is the responsibility of the whole community, and the whole community must monitor our success in achieving the vision set forth in this document."

Bruce Bragg of the Ingham County Health Department believes such a statement could only be made following a vigorous consensus-building process like the one Community Voices instigated. "You must build support for things from within the community," he emphasizes. "Political leaders and other decision makers must believe that they are helping develop things the community supports. Unless you build a base, you can't move forward."

The accountability dimension of the Ingham Action Plan is crucial to the process, according to Bragg and other participants. Lead agencies include local coalitions, established commissions and coordinating agencies, health systems, advocacy and neighborhood organizations, and county boards. Marcus Cheatham, Ingham County health analyst, says that the Action Plan and the Community Voices approach deliver a potent message about the obligations of participation in such a collaborative process. If spoken aloud, he says, the message would be a pull-no-punches statement of expectations based on community interests. "You will be asked to commit substantial resources and change the way you do business," he says. "You will be held accountable by the community in a way you were not before."

People, Not Systems

In focusing on consumers, however, Community Voices project leaders are often struck by the extent to which underserved and uninsured people view health issues not as individual matters, but as part of a family circumstance or larger community issue. Learning how people define family and community can be instructive, they admit. "The difficult thing is listening," says Hakim Farrakhan, corporate operating officer for Bon Secours Baltimore Health System and a Community Voices program leader. "What we understand about family may not apply." In Baltimore's Sandtown-Winchester neighborhoods, Farrakhan says the community's message to health systems has been, "Don't define family to us."

Systems tend to draw lines and qualify the provisions of services to specific groups. But Farrakhan says community people are saying, in essence: "'Don't cherry pick us.' There are programs and services for women, children, seniors – and for men, if they are in pain or using drugs," he continues. "But in early Community Voices focus groups, women in our community would say, 'Our men don't have regular medical care. What are you going to do for them?'" Answering that question led the Community Voices partnership and the Baltimore City Health Department to develop the first full-service Men's Health Center in the United States.

The Nation's First Men's Health Center
When you call the Men's Health Center in Baltimore, the person
answering the phone will most likely say just that: *"Nation's First
Men's Health Center!"* The distinction is an important one, according to acting director Maria Lucas. She and her colleagues –
including staff doctors, the nurse practitioner and physician assistant, medical administrators, counselors, and the Center's outreach
workers – understand that their efforts meet a significant need for
Baltimore men right now. But they also recognize that the Center
is having a ripple effect beyond their community – making history,
in a way, by showing others that it is possible to deliver comprehensive primary health care to a group woefully overlooked in
most communities.

The Center serves uninsured men ages 19 to 64, providing
medical, dental, and behavioral health services. Located near the
Sandtown-Winchester neighborhoods, Lucas says that 90 percent
of patients are African-American men, and the bulk of clients are
between the ages of 38 and 43. "There is no charge for services,"
says Lucas. "And when you tell people that, it's like a cloud is lift-
ed off them. We treat each person with dignity and respect – like
they're worth a million dollars. Isn't that the way we'd all like to
be treated?"

To make the provision of primary care to uninsured men possible, the Center depends on community connections and the
"reconfiguration and reallocation" of traditional funding streams,
Lucas notes. When the facility first opened in April 2000, funding
included support from the Community Voices initiative and other
private funders, state dollars, and existing health department
resources. Now TANF dollars, allocated in an annual lump sum
amount, and capitated payments for Maryland Primary Care
enrollees are the two major sources of funding.

The Center sees 25 to 30 men each day, five days a week –
both patients with scheduled appointments and walk-ins who
come by themselves or with family members. "A lot of men come
for pre-employment physicals," Lucas explains, "including
Baltimore city and county police cadets and construction workers
getting ready to start a new job. Others are young men who need
physicals before entering college. A large number are employed,"
she adds, "but not receiving health care benefits." For these, the
Men's Health Center provides routine care until they can qualify

for some type of coverage, saying, "When they do receive health care benefits through employment, we send a copy of their medical records to the new provider."

Other clients are not employed, however, and arrive without resources or a previous community provider. "Some are just out of correctional facilities and have no source of health care immediately following their release. Many others have not been to a doctor in years. We're seeing very sick people," Lucas says emphatically. The most common diagnoses are hypertension; untreated diabetes and related conditions ("...people at risk of losing toes," she says); prostate concerns; substance abuse issues; and lately, hepatitis C. "We provide comprehensive primary care, laboratory tests, and we have dentistry across the hall where our clients can get a free cleaning and screening for oral health conditions," she continues. "But we are not directly linked to specialty care facilities. So we can test for hepatitis C, but when we get the results, the question is, 'Where do we go from there?'"

"A lot of men come for pre-employment physicals."

—Maria Lucas,
Baltimore

Ms. Lucas and her colleagues initiate a number of steps to access available systems for clients. Until recently, many were eligible for the state indigent care program, Maryland Primary Care, and with such coverage, able to access needed specialty care. But Lucas says that route is temporarily not an option for new patients. "Since November 2001, the Maryland Primary Care program is under an enrollment cap," she explains. "No new enrollees are being accepted and any break in service – not resubmitting the annual application for a Maryland Pharmacy Assistance Program card, for instance – can result in an eligible person being dropped from the program." So Center staff help clients complete the Temporary Emergency Medical and Housing Assistance application if they are eligible, get prescriptions filled through the pharmacy across the street, and look to find specialty care for patients by establishing relationships with providers. "Every hospital in Baltimore City refers to the Men's Health Center," says Lucas. "And we have relationships with particular providers for needed services."

Horacio Sails, the Center's addiction counselor through a Bon Secours substance abuse program on site at the Men's Health Center, coordinated referrals for Center clients until recently. He explains how he and other Men's Health Center staff have worked to form links with local specialty providers to get care for their clients. "If a patient needed cardiology services or follow-up at a gastrointestinal clinic, I would start making calls," says Sails. "'I have a young man who needs this particular service or procedure on a sliding scale or pro bono. Is there a resident who might be available? Is there something we can do for you – somebody you're seeing who needs primary care that we could see?' I would take my business cards and make calls. It's looking for trade-offs and making connections one on one," Sails believes.

"Every hospital in Baltimore City refers to the Men's Health Center."

—Maria Lucas, Baltimore

This level of determination to give Men's Health Center clients the health services they need and deserve has connected the Center with an informal network of local providers. "Everybody knows the need is there," Sails insists. "Lots of good docs are more interested in treating people than anything else. So at first, it was four people a month referred to a local specialty clinic and that turns into 20, people the local clinics – the University of Maryland, Bon Secours, and others – are working in for specialty care." Hardly an ideal system, he admits frankly, but at present, the environment in which the Men's Health Center must function. "The challenge is that health care is not free in this country," he says. "The jobs folks get don't provide health care coverage – maybe some get a little something, but not adequate health care."

But even without coverage, Men's Health Center wraparound services deliver far more than "adequate" health care. "We have found that about 50 percent of our clients have substance abuse issues," Sails notes. "We do assessments to determine if they need detox or other treatments, but we also look at the underlying issues. Depression might be the result of a man working a job that at the end of the week, when he pays all his bills, he has to borrow money to get to and from work the next week. He might have a job, but he needs vocational training to move on." The Men's Health Center links with truck driving schools and computer training centers to help clients "move on" with their lives. "You can see the light come on," says Sails. "The idea changes them when they see there is an opportunity; they can do something different."

The regular Monday and Wednesday afternoon "focus groups" are a kind of facilitated therapy session that gives Center clients a chance to talk through issues and connect with peers and staff. The Center's outreach workers – all males – sit in on the gatherings. Maria Lucas says some Center staff members know firsthand about the difficulties of navigating health systems without insurance coverage from past experience. She adds, however, that since October 2001, all clinical, administrative, and outreach staff members are "full-time civil service employees of the city of Baltimore through the Health Department" – with full benefits, including vacation, sick time, and personal leave. That level of organizational commitment on the part of the Baltimore City Health Department is making it possible for the Center to attract and retain staff and gives a measure of permanence to their collective work.

The outreach worker positions attracted particular community interest, Lucas recalls. "For three community health outreach positions, we had a list of 129 interested applicants!" she remembers. Applicants needed strong interpersonal skills, good verbal and written communication skills, to be well-organized, with a high school diploma or GED, and outreach experience. The gentlemen who were eventually hired handle care coordination and management, follow-up and home visits, and attend health fairs and other community events to reach out to Baltimore City men and potential clients.

The staff of the Men's Health Center also work closely with the Maryland Re-Entry Partnership, a program that case manages people newly released from prison for a three-year period to ensure they receive the health care, employment, and training assistance required to make a successful transition following incarceration. The Men's Health Center has provided health services to approximately 70 percent of all program participants and does monthly outreach to the city's correctional facility.

Traditional wisdom says men are a hard sell when it comes to health care. But Lucas, Sails, and their colleagues are finding that the opposite is true at the Men's Health Center. "So many of the people we see have been through trips to the emergency room and run up those bills," says Lucas. "They've ignored symptoms as long as they could because they couldn't afford medical care." By the time they arrive at the Men's Health Center, she says, they are relieved. "The system is not designed to help," Lucas acknowledges. But she knows the Men's Health Center is. "I hope that from this program, other centers will open," she says with feeling. "We've had visitors from Rochester, New York, and other places. People come to learn how to do what we are doing. When they leave, they say, 'We're going to open 'the nation's second Men's Health Center.'"

Meaningful Involvement in Health Decision Making

The workgroups, committees, and forums Community Voices projects initiate and support are community-specific mechanisms for promoting meaningful involvement in health decision making. In Northern Manhattan, the Difficult to Cover Services Working Group is at the center of a cycle of information gathering and reporting back to the community that is raising complicated service delivery issues and driving the development of solutions to address neglected community mental health issues.

"Breaking down the barriers . . ."
For more than a year, the Working Group pursued a data-development strategy that required interviews with community leaders, mental health providers, and advocates; discussion groups with community people; and an overview of available information about services and demand. In the course of this process, people who used mental health services and community members who did not added their voices to those of physicians, nurses, social workers, and administrators. *Mental Health: The Neglected Epidemic* is the Working Group's report that reflects these diverse perspectives. But the conclusion is unmistakable. As the report states: "...in our community, mental health is perceived as related to all spheres of daily life, not as a medical or psychiatric problem to be treated with medication."

To draw attention to the contents of the report and use it to clarify community issues, attract resources, and prompt action on recommendations, Northern Manhattan Community Voices Collaborative and the Northern Manhattan Mental Health Council jointly sponsored a community forum in May 2001 to release the report. Community-based providers, advocates, researchers, educators, state and city agency representatives, and health system administrators came together to discuss findings. But the level of community interest is sparking more than discussion in Northern Manhattan.

Since the report was released, its recommendations and subsequent community conversations have become part of the Mental Health Council's Planning Committee agenda. Administrators of Northern Manhattan health systems and agencies, mental health providers, researchers, and educators have formed a committee to review the recommendations related to training for primary care providers and community professionals. And the stakeholders who participated in the community forums are part of a feedback committee seeking funding and other opportunities to build capacity for the provision of coordinated care in Northern Manhattan.

"... this whole business of community is ... about developing some concrete, integral relationships with people."

—Moisés Peréz,
New York

Dr. Charlie Corliss, executive director of Inwood Community Services and a member of the Difficult to Cover Services Working Group says, "The Working Group has created a momentum by bringing people together." Moisés Peréz, Northern Manhattan Community Voices Collaborative's director of community services, believes the wider impact of this process is already being felt. "Following these meetings, the executive director of one of the nation's most prestigious research institutions told me that he finally understood what this whole business of community is about," Peréz recalls. "That it is not about the advisory group you bring together, but about developing some concrete, integral relationships with people in the community – going to the community and, more or less, breaking down the barriers that exist between communities and institutions."

Peréz says Northern Manhattan Community Voices Collaborative's determination to investigate community issues and surface community interests in this fashion may result in changes to curriculum, practice, and the allocation of resources – "breakthroughs that will be exemplary for other communities."

Bridging Traditional Divides
The New Mexico "health commons" approach is drawing on community interests to connect physical, oral, and behavioral health services. In Sandoval County, for example, the model is at the

heart of a community effort in Rio Rancho to plan, fund, and construct a facility to house services similar to sites in Bernalillo County. Residents envision a place that would join primary health, behavioral health, dental, and other services with the local food bank, employment and housing offices, early childhood programs, and area nonprofits. A planning committee has sponsored town hall meetings and organized fact-finding visits to Bernalillo County Health Commons sites for architects and planning committee members. Like the Community Voices Shared Solutions work in Doña Ana, Chaves, and Sante Fe Counties, the Sandoval County project is working closely with providers but employing Community Voices strategies to engage the larger community.

This emphasis on a "comprehensive, integrated health commons model" is in response to community desires and requires not just co-location, but broad-based collaboration according to Dan Derksen. "The health commons approach has expanded the number of partners drawn into the conversation – including public health, health care for the homeless, Indian Health Service, primary care, and emergency care services," he says. Health Commons sites established through Community Voices dialogues in one county are shaping the conversation in other places and across the state. "The offshoots of bringing individuals and groups together to work on a particular issue are gaining momentum," Derksen says. "The access and public health issues being raised in local health councils are emerging in medical society and department of health discussions. Enough people have been working together over the last three years that when you convene a group for any reason, they talk about a lot of other issues."

Commenting on the impact of UNM Care, the Community Voices expanded coverage and care program that introduced the health commons approach, Arthur Kaufman, chair of the University of New Mexico Department of Family and Community Medicine, emphasizes the impact at the institutional level. "One of the most important outcomes has been the bridges it has built between the primary care departments – virtually all of our primary care clinics are interdisciplinary including family medicine, internal medicine and/or pediatrics – and the bridges it has built between the University and the safety net practice community," Kaufman states. "Community Voices helped us build a consortium of all six safety net provider organizations in central New Mexico."

A Sustainable System for Language Services

The County of Alameda Uninsured Survey (CAUS) has helped Oakland Community Voices highlight the community interests inherent in language access for people with limited English proficiency in health care and human services. "Of those enrolled in Alliance Family Care (Alameda Alliance for Health's health care coverage product for low-income families), only 12 percent speak English as their primary language," according to Tomiko Connor of Oakland Community Voices. One key recommendation of the CAUS report was to ensure language access in outreach and enrollment as well as health services delivery. The tough part, Connor admits, is financing. "Financing continues to be the key to how you create a sustainable system for language services – interpretation and translation," she says. "Information gathering is part of the groundwork for building a sustainable system."

Community clinics have a wealth of experience in providing culturally and linguistically appropriate care. They often hire community people who speak the languages of their clients and understand how to reach target populations. Oakland Community Voices key partners are guiding efforts to make language access a top priority as they educate policymakers and other decision makers. Connor has been appointed to serve on the statewide Culturally and Linguistically Competent Physicians and Dentists Task Force. The group is developing recommendations for standards, continuing education requirements, and certification of California doctors and dentists.

Yet one reason language-access services are so seldom available, according to Oakland Community Voices partners, is that the services are not generally reimbursable under existing payment streams. An Executive Order signed by President Clinton in 2000 and related standards issued by the U.S. Department of Heath and Human Services Office of Minority Health later that year helped to clarify provider responsibilities with regard to language access. Those actions raised the profile of language access, but did little to create a sense of urgency.

To broaden awareness and catalyze action, Oakland Community Voices joined with The California Endowment and the California HealthCare Foundation to sponsor a roundtable discussion. Alameda County created an immigrant liaison position to help address cultural and linguistic competency barriers to enrollment for state low-income coverage programs. Oakland Community Voices also works closely with the Association of Asian Pacific Community Health Organizations and the California Primary Care Association, organizations taking the lead on language access advocacy on the national and state levels.

Beyond Health

Community Voices participants know that community interests extend beyond the parameters of health, no matter how broadly the term is defined. Housing, employment, transportation, education, justice, opportunity – these are some of the many factors that determine how healthy a community can become. Through their systematic efforts to reach and engage underserved community members and infuse health system discussions and decisions with the community's hard-won insights, Community Voices program leaders believe that a fundamental reorientation is in progress.

Marcus Cheatham, Ingham County health analyst, offers an analogy to explain the depth of change possible through this type of reorientation: "If you are the dog catcher, you can no longer say, 'Hey, I spent all day driving around catching dogs. I've done my bit.' You will be asked to help reduce dog bites, participate in monitoring vector-born disease, organize spay and neuter clinics, and learn how to treat animals in captivity ethically. You won't be a dog catcher anymore," Cheatham concludes. "You'll be an animal health expert!"

Denver Health CEO Patricia Gabow says, "The value of the Community Voices approach is to broaden the scope of solutions and strategies. The essential element is to think beyond the walls of the medical center." A Denver Health Employer-Assisted Home Loan Program is doing just that and illustrates how responding to community interests can take health organizations in unexpected directions.

In January 2001, Denver Health introduced a program to help employees purchase their own homes. Partnering with Fannie Mae, the Colorado Housing Assistance Corporation, Bank One, and First Horizon, Denver Health created a mechanism to allow an employee to borrow up to one-half the balance of his or her retirement account to help pay the down payment or closing costs on a home purchase. Repayment is made through payroll deduction, making it possible for working people in the Denver Health community to own homes sooner than they might have been able to using traditional savings. In the program's first year, 40 employees purchased homes. Denver Health is one of only a handful of health systems across the country offering employees home loan assistance as part of their benefit package. "The idea came from a Community Voices meeting," Elizabeth Whitley says simply – another example of how systems can change and grow when they create mechanisms for learning from communities.

Hakim Farrakhan sees evidence that Community Voices efforts to amplify community voice is building stronger safety nets in specific communities and reorienting perspectives on a broader level. Take the Men's Health Center, for instance. "The Men's Health Center has become a model for efforts in Rochester and elsewhere," he says. "The Men's Health Center staff are driving the development of a specialty and identifying issues related to the health care needs of people coming out of prisons," he adds. "What they are learning is fueling advocacy in Baltimore and statewide" – an emphasis that is prompting discussions in health system board rooms, state agencies, and legislative halls.

"Community Voices is a part of all this," Farrakhan concludes.

Chapter 6:
Learning Laboratories Explore Strategies and Gather Data to Leverage New Resources

- *"Flyers don't work. You give a lot of flyers and people don't come. Going to the church is better, because that's where the people are."* –Outreach worker's explanation of a strategy for reaching neighborhood uninsured.

- *"It's good to enroll people. I like working in the Dominican and Latino communities. You know there is a need and you are part of the solution. There is a feeling of family at work."* –Enrollment worker trained as a promotora, a community health worker.

- The case manager tells the story of a man who refused to go to the doctor because, as he told his wife, there was "nothing wrong" with him. But during a home visit, he learned about a health coverage program he qualified for, and the case manager helped fill out the application and coaxed him into "only one doctor's appointment." At the appointment, he learned he had diabetes and hypertension – "more or less a walking time bomb," to use the case manager's expression. But today he's a different story, she says, changed because "he's learned to take care of himself. He has lost weight, quit drinking his gallon of whole milk a day, and cut down from three packs a day to one." She says no one is more surprised than his wife!

  Strategies like these are making it possible for Community Voices to accomplish what some say is almost impossible.

- *"Our case managers needed a low-cost, user-friendly tool to bridge the communication gap between ourselves and our patients, patient families, and the care team both inside and outside the hospital. Canopy centralizes all data and information in a single, secure database."* –Health system outcomes manager talking about the tracking technology that has reduced hospitalization costs and improved care management for underserved patients.

Strategies like these are making it possible for Community Voices to accomplish what some say is almost impossible – to connect with hard-to-reach people in low-income communities and draw them into existing coverage and care programs. Most safety net providers would be hard-pressed to replicate Community Voices accomplishments within existing systems. As learning laboratories in the *Community Voices: HealthCare for the Underserved* initiative, the 13 sites have invested considerable resources – time, personnel, funding – to form partnerships capable of expanding access to coverage and care. But the methods they employ and the pains they take to learn from the process are sketching out an overarching strategy with the potential to leverage support for fragile safety net systems.

Making Contact, Coordinating Care, and Measuring Results

Community Voices is finding that outreach, enrollment, and care coordination and management are invaluable tools for reaching underserved community members. In the

Many project efforts have led to the development of new technology and tracking mechanisms.

process, many project efforts have led to the development of new technology and tracking mechanisms – capabilities that furnish useful information to safety net providers and state-level decision makers about the scope of issues, community desires, and outcomes achieved.

By combining programmatic approaches and rigorous documentation, Community Voices partners are clarifying the extent of community needs and leveraging resources to expand coverage and care for the underserved. Each Community Voices project is pursuing methods tailored to the interests and resources of their stakeholders, making approaches in North Carolina very different from programs in Washington, D.C., or El Paso. But viewed as a network, the learning laboratories' work reinforces the value of investing in outreach, enrollment, and care management to expand access, measure results, and leverage resources capable of sustaining the work.

Beyond Marketing: Health System Change
and Measurable Results

By and large, health systems are centralized organizations that concentrate resources within facilities to make them more cost-effective and efficient. To access resources, people in need of treatment and extensive care must come inside of health system "walls." Hospital staff and system insiders acclimate to the settings and language of these environments. Community people generally are less comfortable, however. Many otherwise confident people are daunted by the halls of health care. They feel like outsiders as they try to navigate places and ways foreign to them. So they avoid entering if they can.

This "fish out of water" reaction to hospitals is not unique to health systems, of course. The same could be said for human services systems, academic institutions, and many other organizational settings. And to overcome such perceptual barriers and connect with appealing markets, many health systems routinely conceive and mount strategic approaches to reach untapped markets. Outpatient facilities and physician practices in suburban areas are examples of effective strategies to target particular groups or regions and draw people into systems of care. To attract middle class expectant mothers – and eventually attract their families as patients too – health systems may offer classes, orientation sessions, and fitness programs. Similar approaches target emerging markets – baby boomers as they enter menopause, middle-aged children of aging parents, and retirees.

But when it comes to health care for the underserved, few systems market their services quite so aggressively – and safety net providers seldom have the resources required to undertake traditional marketing efforts. Those that do often find that tried-and-true marketing approaches miss the mark when it comes to connecting low-income families, people of color, immigrants, homeless, and others in need of care with existing services. People who have good reason to be wary of government offices or institutions representing authority and those who do not speak English readily need more than billboards and brochures to feel safe asking questions about coverage programs or local health care services.

The perceptions that keep underserved people from appropriately seeking health care and coverage represent a significant barrier to expanding access – one that Community Voices projects have encountered, recognized, and confronted in varying forms. To combat these barriers, Community Voices projects have learned, as one health system manager says, "not just to care for the people who arrive at our door, but to care *before* they arrive."

"People go to church or the laundromat, but they don't come to us"
That lament might be heard in many places – health care systems, health departments, public agencies, and human services offices among them. Community Voices participants believe the surest way to engage underserved people is a twofold process – to go where they are and work hand in hand with community organizations they already trust. Churches, community centers, and schools are likely places in many communities, but in some neighborhoods, the best places might be beauty salons, street corners, clubs, and pool halls. The important thing is the opportunity to reach people and the level of trust in the connection.

In Ingham County, Community Voices has turned to specific organizations to learn from and engage hard-to-reach populations. Although early community forums attracted many participants, African Americans, Latinos, and Native Americans were not well represented in the dialogues. The relative absence of these voices reduced the relevance of the recommendations, prompting a more targeted approach to draw those missing into the conversation. Working closely with Ingham Community Voices, the Mestizo Anishnabe Health Alliance and the African American Health Institute sponsored summits to help widen the circle.

Brenda Evans, of the Greater Lansing African American Health Institute, believes the collaboration has improved outreach in a way that benefits both Community Voices and the Institute. "We do educational outreach related to health disparities. Our mission is focusing on total health – physical, mental, and spiritual dimensions. Through Community Voices, we are not just bringing the African-American community together, but connecting that discussion to the larger community conversation about health, mutual health issues, and the resources available. Community Voices created a space to do that." The educational outreach is increasing connections and partnerships "with public agencies, health systems, and other organizations trying to reach out to the African-American community and vice versa," Evans explains.

In October 2001, the Institute partnered with Ingham County's two major health systems and local health ministry organizations representing both African-American and white faith communities to sponsor a conference for the health and faith communities on "Health, Wholeness, and Change." She notes that the conference crossed many barriers – between health and community, across denominational lines, and racial barriers as well. "I've seen connections that would not have been made without Community Voices outreach efforts."

Consumer Health Access Teams (CHAT) are facilitating connections between health and human services systems in Washington, D.C., and uninsured community people. The Community Voices Collaborative of the District of Columbia works through CHAT to conduct outreach and enrollment into the D.C. HealthCare Alliance program for eligible low-income residents.

CHAT are coordinated through a community-based, grassroots organization – the East Capital Center for Change. "Four four-person teams are made up of community members who were or are users of the public health care system," says Judith Johnson, director of the D.C. Community Voices Collaborative. "They concentrate their efforts in three D.C. wards, talking with people at emergency rooms, local businesses, and churches, in laundromats or on buses – anywhere in the neighborhood." Johnson says CHAT use a web-based system for tracking their contacts. "They track the number of people they talk to, the locations they visit, the number of people they accompany to enrollment sites and assist, and the complexity of their health issues," Johnson explains adding, "They are also in the process of developing a tracking mechanism for stories."

Frontline Workers and Product Success
Irene Ibarra, CEO of the Alameda Alliance for Health, says, "The community clinics in Alameda County – Asian Health Services, La Clinica, and their sister clinics in the Access to Care Coalition – have been the front line of outreach and enrollment. They consistently find a way to assist families and they do it in places families frequent – not government offices, but familiar neighborhood clinics." Considering how many uninsured people are "'blended families' from an immigration status perspective," Ibarra says that is no small feat.

"Our model from the beginning was comprehensive, seamless coverage for families. So the outreach-enrollment approach is 'anyone who needs health and dental coverage, we'll find the program they qualify for.' To the family," Ibarra emphasizes, "it looks seamless. They have one place to go and they are all covered."

From an operations perspective, however, she says what the community center network is accomplishing is complicated and groundbreaking.

"They take the time – face to face, on a one-on-one basis – to explain things to applicants."

—Irene Ibarra, Alameda County

"The county social services worker sits side by side with the community health center enrollment person and together they determine eligibility up front – regardless of the applicant family's immigration status," Ibarra explains. "Whether it's a public program or a product designed to fill the gap, such as Family Care, the family is able to access a full range of programs at one place. And they take the time – face to face, on a one-on-one basis – to explain things to applicants. People who haven't had insurance before, many who speak another language, with family members of varying citizenship status – they understand about the need for insurance and they buy it."

According to Ibarra, Family Care's enrollment is due to the Access for Care Coalition's outreach strategies. "The product success of Family Care is due to front-line folks," she says emphatically. "Their efforts are so much more effective than marketing campaigns. The lesson we learned with Family Care is that if it's affordable and offered by a trusted community person, families will pay premiums for health insurance." Ibarra adds that the success of the Alameda outreach-enrollment model is being replicated elsewhere in the county and across the state as human service and health care agencies see how effective it can be.

Language Access to Reduce System Barriers

Language services in community clinics make it possible for outreach and enrollment workers to have in-depth, one-on-one question-and-answer sessions with potential applicants. In Alameda County, where so many different languages are spoken by such a large proportion of the population, the network of community clinics take language access as a given in reaching uninsured.

Asian Health Services, for example, hires outreach workers fluent in Cantonese, Vietnamese, and Korean. Yet even in communities in which few speak another language, Community Voices is addressing language access gaps to expand outreach and enrollment.

"We had a difficult time getting our arms around the magnitude of our communication problems with people who had limited English, since many interactions were reported as individual cases," says Lisa Hartsock talking about FirstHealth Community Voices efforts in North Carolina. "The reported numbers in the census were so small, that the data did not justify making language access a focus. Plus, the number of reported incidents were few – probably because people were fearful or inexperienced with the system," she admits.

"But this was something many people knew was a problem even though we couldn't provide immediate documentation. So we have moved to educate staff about the availability of the language-line service that we use with speaker phones. We created cultural sensitivity classes so health system staff as well as health department and social services agency workers can better understand and address barriers. And we started Spanish-language training for staff." Hartsock describes this as "reflective of the health system's ability to adjust to the needs of the community." She says enrollment in the classes is increasing and the enhanced awareness of barriers for even a small number of North Carolina consumers is good for the system as a whole.

Outreach Workers: A New Cadre of Community Experts

Outreach workers – the community people who expand access to health coverage and care by providing information, education, and assistance to uninsured and underserved in their neighborhoods – are emerging as an essential element in many Community Voices enrollment strategies. In Baltimore, the city has created a community health outreach worker civil service position – establishing a training curriculum, standards, and certification program that are elevating the position in the eyes of applicants as well as other city workers. But in many communities, outreach workers are an afterthought

In Baltimore, the city has created a community health outreach worker civil service position.

seldom, if ever, drawn into the organizational structures of health and human services systems. By contrast, Community Voices projects are illustrating the value of recruiting and supporting the development of community health outreach workers. By emphasizing training, networking, and tracking, many Community Voices collaborations are making the case for community health workers being part of the health care team.

Promotoras: The Backbone of Outreach and Enrollment
Through Northern Manhattan Community Voices, Alianza Domincana, Inc., and the Columbia University Mailman School of Public Health collaborated to develop a curriculum and training program for health outreach workers. The training sessions not only prepare participants to assist in completing application forms to facilitate enrollment in public programs, but also help develop culturally-sensitive communication skills and outreach strategies. More than 20 community-based organizations have participated in the training – turning their staff and volunteers into a corps of outreach and enrollment resource persons available at day care centers, housing advocacy organizations, school-based clinics, domestic violence shelters, faith-based services, and other community sites throughout Northern Manhattan neighborhoods.

Based on the Community Voices centrally-coordinated training program and the collaborative's extensive network of connections across the community, the Northern Manhattan partners secured a New York State enrollment contract. With the training program as a basis, Alianza Dominica worked with an additional 20 women to prepare them to act as "promotoras" – health outreach workers in Latino communities – as part of the Welfare to Employment Program. Talking to their peers in area neighborhoods, promotoras make follow-up calls, help set up appointments, and invite people they meet to seek more information at Alianza's Center for Health Promotion and Education. These local health workers are the backbone of Northern Manhattan Community Voices outreach and enrollment efforts in Washington Heights-Inwood and Central Harlem. In 2000, their efforts were responsible for 43 percent of all families enrolled in coverage programs.

Sandra Harris of Northern Manhattan Community Voices says that, in addition to the six-part training at the outset, the twice-a-year updates are ongoing. "New rules continue to come up and the community-based organizations hire new staff, making periodic training a necessity," she explains. "Given the recent catastrophic events in New York – September 11th and Flight 58 – we have been operating in a very reactive mode. Outreach and enrollment's workload has tripled" – an example of how quickly a community can come to depend on the information and services trusted local promotoras provide.

Local Outreach and State-Level Discussions
Renate Pore, director of the Governor's Cabinet on Children and Families, knows that trust is the essential element in reaching rural residents too. "The Family Resource Networks (FRNs) in place are really about building trust," she says. "In West Virginia, resources are limited. The same people participate all the time." Regional Family Resource Networks are grassroots organizations dedicated to improving local services to children and families. By working through FRNs, Community Voices efforts connect with those trusted people and provide them with the resources to reach uninsured families in their areas. But Community Voices also takes pains to connect work in remote communities with statewide efforts to inform the implementation of policies – "to connect rural areas to the rest of the world," Pore says.

West Virginia Community Voices partnerships made it possible for local coalitions to develop training materials and conduct outreach-enrollment training for Regional Family Resource Network staff, Children's Health Insurance Program (CHIP) outreach workers, and community activists across the state. The development of the training manual represented a joint effort involving the West Virginia Welfare Reform Coalition, the American Friends Service Committee, Appalachian Legal Services, and Community Voices.

Working closely with the statewide Healthy Kids Coalition, Community Voices tools were placed in the hands of trusted local people. As a result, outreach workers made tremendous headway in enrolling the state's CHIP and Medicaid-eligible children. Through the Healthy Kids Coalition, enrollment issues and barriers in remote, rural regions were connected to state-level discussions. FRN outreach workers and CHIP personnel attended Healthy Kids Coalition meetings with state agency representatives.

"Just sitting around the table together saved a lot of time," notes Community Voices' Nancy Tolliver.

Results to date indicate that the network of connections and resources Community Voices facilitated has been productive. More than 40,000 West Virginia children have been enrolled – 93 percent of eligible children in 2001 according to state data. "The challenge now is re-enrollment," says Tolliver. "It appears that families do not re-enroll their children for CHIP when the year membership is up." The Healthy Kids Coalition is taking that issue seriously and working to find ways to circumvent this emerging barrier. As it does, Community Voices continues to support connections between trusted local outreach workers and state-level deliberations.

Many Community Access Points

Community Voices El Paso has used a multi-tiered strategy to focus local energy and resources on outreach and enrollment. Hospital staff, community promotoras, and other outreach workers; a 24-hour call line (*La Linea de Salud*); and 40 community-based organizations are all part of a broad-based effort to ensure that eligible community members have access to available programs. According to Thomason Hospital's Pete Duarte, Community Voices El Paso has provided the legwork, staff work, training, and resources to draw the community together and keep so many diverse activities on track. But he sums up the principle behind every aspect of the strategy by saying, "It's nothing less, nothing more than getting people to trust you."

To that end, Community Voices provides training and information to prepare outreach workers at a number of key access points. Hospital staff handling patient discharge are completing applications before people leave the hospital and often getting them enrolled the same day. The bilingual registered nurses who staff *La Linea de Salud* 24 hours a day, seven days a week, answer questions and relay people who may be eligible for coverage programs to Community Voices promotoras for follow-up. Trained outreach workers from the nonprofits and community agencies participating in the West Texas CHIP Collaborative facilitate outreach and enrollment in neighborhoods throughout the region. Through an innovative mechanism designed to strengthen local nonprofits and expand enrollment, community-based organizations receive a financial incentive for successful outreach and enrollment efforts. The program provides "very modest compensation for their efforts," according to Duarte. "But it is money that goes to people in the community, and we are a region with a chronic unemployment problem."

The overall impact of this cycle of activity is strengthening nonprofits, building an infrastructure to connect the resources of community organizations with safety net providers, and increasing the number of low-income people with access to coverage and care. In the process, Community Voices is changing how community members access health systems, according to Gale Morrow, deputy regional director of the Texas Department of Health, Regions 9 and 10. "The outreach process teaches low-income adults how to use health insurance and the medical system," she says. "If Community Voices can help community members learn to use primary care physicians before going to the emergency room, it helps save money and helps the enrolled get the kind of care they need when they need it."

"It's nothing less, nothing more than getting people to trust you."

—*Pete Duarte,*
El Paso

The emphasis on enrollment also is helping Thomason Hospital, the county's tertiary care facility, identify uninsured who access emergency services often – "frequent flyers" as they are called in many hospitals. These individuals are part of a case management program in the works that assesses the costs and benefits of interventions with this population to guide future investments.

Care Management and Coordination of Resources
Understanding the costs and benefits inherent in managing care and coordinating the use of health system resources is a stream of work Community Voices projects are exploring in a number of ways.

The Voices of Detroit Initiative (VODI) screens all new enrollees to the VODI program to identify people with hypertension, diabetes, cancer, asthma, or more than three visits to local emergency departments in a single year. Any one of those factors will place a new enrollee with one of VODI's Care Management Teams. VODI's Lucille Smith says, "Each team is assigned four or five VODI primary sites in a set geographic area within the city of

Detroit. This supports the concept of establishing a 'medical home' for the client – something that is paramount in the VODI program and provides primary care providers a point person when referring a client to Care Management or other services." Care Management Teams work with all providers within their territory, making them valuable resources for understanding the scope and depth of health care services provided by various VODI partners.

VODI Care Management Teams – made up of a registered nurse and community outreach worker – do home visits, connect clients with other services, provide health education, and identify transportation or related issues (housing, employment, food assistance) that affect a person's ability to manage or improve health conditions. Care Management social workers assist teams as needed to refer clients for mental health or substance abuse treatment. All members of the team center activities on a treatment plan, developed in cooperation with the client. "Health is viewed as a continuum in the VODI system of care," Smith explains. "Care Management assists the client any time he or she moves from one end of the continuum to the other."

From a safety net perspective, Smith says the Care Management Teams approach is providing information about the relative costs and outcomes of such a comprehensive intervention strategy. Overall, VODI tracking and assessment of services is providing information about utilization of outpatient and inpatient services and insurance status. But Smith notes that Care Management Teams are producing additional qualitative data and identifying activities that can fill health gaps in unexpected ways. "What they are learning from clients is helping us put together health education and other classes based on population need," she says. "One Care Management Team has developed a resume-writing class, for instance. They are finding so many people who want to work, but are trapped in low-paying jobs or unemployed. So the team is focusing on employment assistance and building a website with job information." Care Management Teams also identify short-term unmet needs – like glucose strips for diabetics or blood pressure cuffs for people with hypertension. "We are making it possible for clients to have access to these tools," Smith adds, "to help them monitor their health conditions and make sure they have what they need to take care of themselves."

Tracking, Care Management, and New Technology

Community Voices projects are using outreach, enrollment, and care management activities to springboard the development of new technology to support better tracking and use of health system resources. These new technologies are expanding the capacity of safety net providers and helping Community Voices partners learn more from outreach and enrollment activities underway in their communities.

In North Carolina, the FirstHealth Community Voices case management program depends on a web-based system called Canopy. Canopy was developed as a case management tool for managing the care of patients with chronic illness across integrated health services delivery systems. The secure system makes it possible for clinicians at multiple sites to record and share clinical, administrative, and outcomes information about individual patients. FirstConnection, the Community Voices pilot program for managing the care of 200 previously uninsured clients – some with serious health conditions – uses the Canopy system. Cindy McNeill-McDonald, FirstHealth's director of outcomes, says that Canopy's common database "has been our saving grace."

> *"A lot of patients out there in the community, especially in rural areas, don't know how to navigate our system."*
>
> —*Anissa Chapman, North Carolina*

With Canopy in physician offices as well as outpatient and inpatient facilities, McNeill-McDonald notes that case managers "can access all the information we need with a click of a computer mouse." Since FirstConnection participants receive preventive care, primary care, specialty care, and prescription drugs along with case management support, tracking services in relation to goals for each client is essential to learning from the pilot program. At the same time, FirstHealth case managers are getting a better handle on hidden barriers. As Case Manager Anissa Chapman notes: "We feel we are providing lots of services. But a lot of patients out there in the community, especially in rural areas, don't know how to navigate our system. Once we learned that, we were able to help."

Chapman points to services and education available for people with diabetes, as an example. "We had 16 people in the program who were diabetics, but prior to enrollment, none of them had any education related to diabetes." Since enrolling in FirstConnection, 15 have completed education programs and 62 percent have their diabetes under control. Chapman remembers one client in particular.

A 66-year-old woman with diabetic complications severe enough to require hospitalization was enrolled in FirstConnection. When Chapman made a home visit, she found her living in a singlewide trailer – her home for more than 30 years. "There were holes in the floor and holes in the ceiling where she had hung her lights. No phone, so my only contact was monthly home visits," she recalls. Behind in doctor bills already, the woman's minimum-wage job had made most health care beyond her means. "She couldn't afford medications, and she didn't understand the purpose of them. But she was proud of what she did have, proud of her independence," Chapman explains. Following enrollment in the program, the client received diabetes education. "She is going to the doctors and getting her medication monthly. Her diabetes and blood pressure are under control. And because we have educated this lady," Chapman says with pride, "she is in control of her medical regimen and able to take better care of herself."

FirstHealth CEO Charles T. Frock believes the combination of technology and case management is providing some useful lessons. "A lot of health systems overlook the potential of case management to reduce costs. With Canopy, we saw an opportunity to do the right thing, to do it better, and to save money along the way." Community Voices' Lisa Hartsock adds that FirstConnection experience and use of Canopy throughout FirstHealth is laying important groundwork for the development of care management in the region. "We are really still working at a case-management level," she notes. "FirstHealth and local agencies have initiated discussions recently about the barriers faced by people who access services from many different health care and human service agencies throughout the area. A pilot project of service integration in one small community would allow public and private partners to provide services as one unit – and would require shared information, resources, and standards of care." Hartsock acknowledges the "enormity" of such a model and admits discussions are in an early stage. "But it is a step in the direction of the ultimate goal – care management."

> "With Canopy, we saw an opportunity to do the right thing, to do it better, and to save money along the way."
>
> —Charles Frock,
> North Carolina

Combining Outreach, Enrollment, Tracking, and Case Management to Improve Health Outcomes for Underserved

Denver Health Community Voices is combining a targeted outreach strategy involving Community Health Advisors; new technology to track enrollment; and a randomized, controlled case management study to reach and learn from underserved community members while expanding access to coverage and care.

Community Health Advisors (CHAs) – the outreach workers who connect with underserved Denver residents in selected neighborhoods – are the most visible elements in Community Voices' overall efforts. CHAs, many of whom live in the neighborhoods they serve, bring information about health services and coverage programs to community organizations, centers, businesses, and churches. "The goal is to provide culturally-sensitive outreach," explains Elizabeth Whitley of Denver Health Community Voices. "We undertake community outreach not only to increase enrollment in available programs, but to provide information and resources to help communities assume greater responsibility for their own health."

"A full day's work…"

On some days, CHAs connect with Community Partners visiting Denver organizations, schools, and churches to make presentations, answer questions, and connect local residents to health care resources. On other days, CHAs work one-on-one with community members in need of immediate assistance – like the day Andrea Garcia helped a 17-year-old homeless girl who was pregnant. Making it possible for the young woman to access medical care was only the first step, Garcia recalls. "While she was being given a thorough prenatal exam, I began calling our community partners looking for a place for her to sleep that night. As I was calling, it dawned on me how fortunate I was to know where I would be sleeping and eating that evening," Garcia remembers. "This thought strengthened my resolve not to leave her until I knew she had somewhere to sleep besides her car."

In the end, Garcia was successful – finding not only a place for one night, but for many nights, at a home for pregnant teens. "She interviewed with them over the phone," says Garcia, "and they accepted her for an 18-month program that would help her get a good job and get back on her feet after she delivered." Garcia acknowledges that assistance like this can be "a full day's work for everything to fall into place." But she says it is well worth the effort.

Building a Pipeline for Community Outreach Workers
Through Denver Health Community Voices, community partners and health system decision makers are recognizing a pivotal role for outreach workers like Andrea Garcia in the health care team. In an informal survey of CHA Community Partners, partners indicate they are impressed with the quality of outreach and how it is bridging between health systems and community organizations to help local residents. To ensure that Denver has access to a capable workforce of community outreach workers, Denver Health Community Voices partnered with the local community college to launch a new endeavor.

As Whitley explains, "Initially, CHAs' training, orientation, and continuing education were done internally, but we wanted to provide more comprehensive workplace and vocational training and field experience. So we collaborated with the Community College of Denver to create a 17-credit hour training program." The Community Health Worker Certificate Program takes one or two semesters to complete and is open to community members with a high school diploma or GED. All the benefits of community college enrollment – cooperative education, financial aid and scholarships, and job placement assistance – are available to Certificate Program graduates. The first class graduated in May 2002.

Redesigning Enrollment
To strengthen the local safety net, Denver Health Community Voices has made increased enrollment a target – both to reduce uncompensated care and draw eligible people into coverage programs. Accomplishing that required a complete redesign in the enrollment process, according to Whitley. "Enrollment specialists are at every Denver Health site in the community," she explains. And they have the skills to connect with a wide range of underserved Denver residents. "Sixteen of our 31 specialists are fluent in

Spanish," Whitley says. "Two speak French, and we have people who speak Vietnamese, Portuguese, Russian, and a number of Nigerian and Senegalese dialects." Perhaps just as importantly, the enrollment applications have been simplified. Working closely with Denver Department of Human Services and other public agencies, Denver Health Community Voices has produced some impressive results. Almost 75,000 people were enrolled by the end of 2000, generating nearly $38 million in revenues as payment for health care services.

The mechanism for tracking all these enrollment applications is called AppTrack. Denver Health developed the windows-based software to make it possible to build a database related to application submission and eligibility determination for public programs. Since it was piloted and refined, AppTrack has been made available to the Denver Department of Human Services, Colorado Access (the state's Medicaid managed care organization), and the Colorado Community Health Network. "A new project in Colorado Springs plans to widen the use of AppTrack by making it web-based," Whitley adds.

Data Collection to Document Outcomes and Share Lessons
Case management is another opportunity for learning from Community Voices efforts to expand access to care in Denver. In July 1999, Denver Health Community Voices began a two-year, randomized study through the Adult Case Management Program. "The Program is designed to demonstrate that case management of chronically ill adults across funding streams and clinical disciplines improves health outcomes and lowers costs," Whitley explains. By tracking services and costs in a treatment group of 52 patients, compared with a control group of 42, Denver Health's case management study is producing data on what types of interventions produce positive patient outcomes – and at what cost.

"Preliminary data show decreased emergency department, detox, and inpatient admissions, along with increased outpatient visits and enhanced quality of life," Whitley reports. Such results have prompted replication of case management studies to continue the learning. "Because of our experience with Denver Health Community Voices, we have replicated the model in other departments and sites and instituted three new case management programs," says Whitley. An emergency room case management program for "frequent users of the emergency department"; a program at the county jail; and a program for patients with physical, behavioral, and substance abuse issues are underway. "The Community Voices Case Management Program is the only one with a randomized controlled study," Whitley notes. "But the methodology for evaluating all programs is the same otherwise." As data is gathered and analyzed, the goal is to share information with key audiences via professional journals, community publications, and internal and state-level reports.

Denver Health Community Voices case management efforts in conjunction with outreach, enrollment, and tracking are identifying issues at the heart of improving health outcomes for vulnerable people. Although clients and case managers speak eloquently about the value of personal connections to draw underserved people into existing programs and help them navigate health systems, case managers and Community Voices partner organizations know that many policy decisions made outside of the community continue to limit what they can accomplish. The undocumented status of many immigrants; the complexity of accessing income and other supports for needy disabled people; the ongoing need for transitional housing; and the limited connections within health systems to link treatment for physical, behavioral, and substance abuse issues emerge as serious barriers to improving health for case management study participants. As these and other obstacles surface, Denver Health Community Voices shares data and stories with state-level decision makers and colleagues nationwide to inform discussions about health resources and needed investments.

Denver Health Community Voices shares data and stories with state-level decision makers and colleagues nationwide.

Whitley credits the Community Voices initiative as responsible in a basic way for making all of this related activity possible. "As a public hospital, we are vigilant about how we spend public money. That makes us somewhat risk averse," she admits. "Community Voices gave us the opportunity to be a learning laboratory – to try new things without that fear."

Do and Document Approach Leverages Resources

Whitley and her colleagues at Community Voices sites across the United States say that sustaining outreach, enrollment, case management, and care coordination beyond the initiative funding period is an important focus of their project efforts. Only limited resources are available for enrollment, and few public programs include payment mechanisms for outreach, care coordination, or case management. Yet these are among the tools they find are essential to reaching underserved community members.

Community Voices program leaders believe their learning laboratory role is helping to make the case for these "added-value" approaches with potential funders in their communities, regionally, and at the state and federal levels. By documenting findings and sharing both results and process lessons, Community Voices projects are furnishing cost-benefit data and other evidence to expand programs and continue the learning. They also are pooling their knowledge – coming together as a network to inform discussions about the allocation of resources to strengthen safety net systems and improve access to coverage and care for the most needy.

In one significant example of the collective impact of Community Voices lessons, the U.S. Health Resource and Service Administration (HRSA) developed its $200 million Community Access Program (CAP) to address many systemic barriers to improving access identified through Community Voices work. Ten Community Voices project sites were selected as CAP recipients. In most cases, the community and health system stakeholders that came together to develop CAP applications were brought to the table by Community Voices efforts. And the community guidance surfaced through Community Voices forums, surveys, and outreach identified the targets for CAP programming – often efforts to expand work already begun through the initiative.

Central New Mexico CAP expands on Community Voices Strategies
In New Mexico, a consortium of all central New Mexico safety net providers came together to apply for the HRSA CAP grant in a process described by key participants as "an important spin-off" of Community Voices collaboration. Arthur Kaufman, chair of the University's Department of Family and Community Medicine,

notes that the provider partners include the University Health Sciences Center, the state department of health, the Indian Health Service in the Albuquerque area, the First Nations Urban Indian Clinic, Healthcare for the Homeless, and First Choice Community Health. "The group built on UNM Care collaboration and successfully applied for the HRSA grant," Kaufman states.

CAP program objectives echo and expand upon the Community Voices targets forged through the New Mexico Shared Solutions approach. As Kaufman says, "The consortium has mounted a redesign program to reduce patient cycle times in the clinics; share vital, protected patient medical information across systems; construct 'one-stop-shopping' services for medical, dental, and behavioral health that includes case management, community outreach workers, and social services; and to sharply increase enrollment of indigent, uninsured patients into a primary care home."

"Our work underscored the need for quick and ready access to information."

—Dan Derksen, New Mexico

Embedded in this array of collaborative work are principles and strategies first explored through Community Voices, says Dan Derksen. A model of care that builds on the assets of community and provider stakeholders; the use of community health workers or promotoras; integration of safety net systems to improve community-responsive care – these are outgrowths of Community Voices lessons, but taken a step further as the work has attracted additional resources. The CAP emphasis on information systems is an example, Derksen believes. "Our work underscored the need for quick and ready access to information," he says. "The technology is there, but confidentiality and other issues have been obstacles. Through this collaborative work, we are sorting through the issues around information interface."

Catherine Thompkins of Affiliated Computer Services, Inc., a collaborating organization working on the Central CAP information system, says the process requires attention to partner needs and concerns across the board. "The ultimate goal is to share patient information among all of the safety net providers," she explains. "Organizations are very protective of their data and we understand that. The technical staffs are particularly protective, and since we come from that environment, we certainly share their concerns." Thompkins notes that provider issues – who delivers

122

what information and how – are being worked through steadily as part of the process.

Scheduling is another critical element of integrating provider resources and expanding access. "We know that many of the people we are trying to identify use the emergency room as their primary care physicians," she continues. "We want to try to attach these folks to primary care providers and try to relieve the pressure on the ERs. We have developed a CAP scheduling system and asked every provider to set aside appointments for CAP patients. With this scheduling system, someone in the ER can log onto the CAP system, determine a clinic that is close to where the patient lives, and schedule him or her for a visit to the clinic as a follow-up to the ER treatment. There are also links in the system to assist in directing patients to social services."

"We developed a CAP scheduling system and asked every provider to set aside appointments for CAP patients."

—Catherine Thompkins, New Mexico

Because Central New Mexico CAP participants includes key state-level collaborating organizations – the state Health Policy Commission and Primary Care Association, for example – issues that surface through the CAP process can be shared with decision makers responsible for the allocation of public and other resources statewide. Collaboration at so many levels is producing some tangible results, Kaufman adds. "By the end of the first year of the CAP grant, our project was considered one of the ten best in the country," he says. "We were refunded for a second year."

Leveraging Resources Deepens Collaboration, Attracts New Partners
In addition to CAP, many Community Voices projects have received additional funding to expand access to needed services through an American Legacy Foundation initiative. In Detroit, VODI is building on collaborative relationships in place to expand services to needy community members. "We've put together smoking cessation classes," explains VODI's Lucille Smith, "but we also are working with pharmacies to provide 'the patch' to people as part of the program."

Collaboration has become the linchpin in Northern Manhattan Community Voices' success at leveraging additional resources to coordinate planning and programming related to asthma. Despite a number of asthma initiatives based in the community, the hospitalization rates among asthma sufferers were not decreasing. Sandra Harris recalls that Community Voices helped raise the question, "Where are these patients coming from?" To find out, Community Voices gathered researchers, health care providers, and community advocates to participate in a mapping exercise – both to better understand the community impact of asthma and share information. "That is the value of Community Voices," Harris believes, "to maximize resources and serve as a neutral participant to promote awareness, service coordination, and education."

Columbia's Mailman School of Public Health emerged as a key partner in Community Voices' work to improve asthma management through provider training and community education. Through efforts to engage asthma initiatives already underway as well as Presbyterian Hospital's Ambulatory Care Network, the Northern Manhattan Improvement Corporation, Alianza Dominicana, Fort George Head Start, and the Community Life Center, Community Voices received a two-year planning grant from the Centers for Disease Control. Sandra Harris says the asthma initiative is a "perfect example" of how Community Voices can generate information to attract support. "Not only can these practices leverage additional resources," she adds, "but the process helps us to better assess why the care is not being coordinated and where there are barriers that need to be overcome. This can only happen when you have the people around the table who bring different pieces of the health delivery puzzle."

Community Voices connections are finding ways to leverage additional resources to expand the scope of their work and keep learning from these promising strategies. And the level of interest from other private philanthropies, state-level organizations, and federal agencies is gratifying. But program leaders in every Community Voices site freely admit that these are steps along a continuum – pieces of a larger puzzle they hope to help solve over time. They know that the resources needed to expand and sustain care and coverage for the underserved are, at present, far greater than any community can attract, no matter how credible the evidence of impact. As one Community Voices participant says frankly, "I worry about sustainability each and every day."

Chapter 7:
Leadership, Partnerships, Relationships – Enduring Connections Across Communities

At the Community Voices Miami Multi-Agency Consortium (MAC) meetings, the representative of a neighborhood agency serving newly arrived immigrants would sit next to a senior administrator from the local health system. In some respects, Marta Pizarro's agency in East Little Havana was a world away from Joseph Rogers' office at Jackson Health System. But after working side by side at MAC meetings, Marta and Joseph heard each other's points of view and were able to recognize their similarities as well as differences. When community people raised concerns about the operation of Jackson's satellite clinic in Little Havana, Marta shared them with Joseph and he offered to sit in on a clinic board meeting. Community Voices Miami's Leda Perez says that this connection is typical of how conversations initiated around the MAC table are being continued in other venues across the community. More than 90 agencies are linked to the Consortium. They represent hospitals, community-based groups, research institutions, government bodies, churches, and local coalitions. Perez says they come together "to mediate a discussion on health care." But health care is not the only subject under discussion. "The relationships have led to more than just an action plan," Perez believes. "Community Voices has made it personal. We tend to think of institutions as if they were empty halls. We forget about the people." By bringing people from a wide range of agencies to the same table, she sees evidence that participants are beginning to understand and appreciate the perspectives of fellow MAC members. Outside of the meetings, members are drawing on these connections to pursue individual organizational objectives as well as common Community Voices pursuits.

The *Community Voices: HealthCare for the Underserved* initiative is responsible for substantive, measurable change in many communities – expanded coverage for previously uninsured people, greater access to health care services for underserved community members, increases in the enrollment of eligible people for programs targeting low-income families, and dental care for greater numbers of poor people, to name a few examples. But Community Voices program leaders report that other, less obvious changes are taking place in their communities as a result of the initiative – changes occurring within individuals, between participants, and across communities of interest. As important as expanded access to health coverage and care are to underserved people today, the leadership, partnerships, and relationships making such change possible holds even greater promise for tomorrow.

Community Voices collaboration is spurring leaders across communities, regions, and states to work with their counterparts in health systems, nonprofit organizations, universities, dental clinics, and public agencies. Community Voices forums and outreach efforts have provided a venue for community people to step forward and assume active roles in health care discussions and decision making. Advisory groups, boards, and new collaborative structures are furnishing the infrastructure to bring diverse interests together and sustain fledgling connections. As a result, interpersonal and organizational links between and among health care professionals, hospital managers, pastors, university professors, public administrators, and neighborhood spokespersons are establishing relationships that bridge the chasms often separating practice, education, research, and community.

Greater Diversity, Changing Perceptions Signify Community Impact

The nexus of these connections is the work at hand – expanded access to coverage and care for underserved people in their communities. But the experience of successful collaboration is changing individual participants and beginning to reshape the perceptions and principles guiding health system decision making in some communities. The ability to accomplish things believed to be too difficult, to overcome barriers considered insurmountable, to raise issues too long overlooked, is converting reluctant participants and emboldening people with a passion for improving the well-being of communities.

Transformations are taking place at the personal level as perceptions change within individuals based on experiences. At the community level, the faces of participants reflect broader transformations in progress as people of color, immigrants, low-income workers, and other underserved community members join with health system administrators and organizational representatives to participate in Community Voices focus groups, meetings, and forums. The diversity of people participating in advisory and decision-making bodies – their ethnic, racial, and income diversity as well as important differences in life experience – are reshaping beliefs about who leads and who follows.

Community Voices projects are bringing their collective wisdom and energy to bear on complex and seemingly intractable problems.

Across communities, regions, and states, Community Voices projects are bringing their collective wisdom and energy to bear on complex and seemingly intractable problems as they share lessons and impel others to take action. Community Voices program leaders have no illusions about the policy and practice obstacles yet to be overcome if permanent change in health care is to occur, but they speak often of the value of changes underway in their communities and how remarkable they seem. Although hard to quantify, Community Voices project directors believe that the quality of leadership, partnerships, and relationships in communities may turn out to be the true measure of the initiative's long-term impact.

Skills, Experience, Vision – Leadership Catalyzes Community Voices
Health systems, community organizations, and public institutions need leaders with the skills, experience, and vision to recognize that health care has implications for community well-being beyond the marketplace. The administrators, managers, providers, and advocates leading Community Voices project activities bring considerable skills to their pursuits. Many are health system CEOs, chairs of university departments, administrators of health delivery organizations, and seasoned advocates. Yet Kellogg Foundation program staff knew from past experience that work within traditional circles – health system administrators working only with other hospital CEOs, for instance – was not likely to promote innovative models for expanding health coverage and care for underserved community members. New approaches would need to encompass health system stakeholders from every level of the

community and give decision makers the opportunity to work in concert with individuals from outside their immediate spheres.

Thus, one intention of Community Voices was to make it possible for leaders from a variety of institutions to build on existing skills by giving them the time, resources, and impetus to undertake broad-based collaboration around expanded access to care and coverage. Only through practical experience, Kellogg Foundation program staff reasoned, would participants come to appreciate the perspectives of those outside of their immediate circles and, over time, to trust other problem-solving approaches. To that end, Community Voices tapped a wide range of organizational partners from health systems, community organizations, advocacy groups, and academic institutions.

Within that framework, Community Voices project directors report that the initiative is developing the expertise and deepening the commitment of many visionary individual leaders. In turn, these leaders are raising issues, attracting new resources, and forging connections to sustain Community Voices programming, policy education, and advocacy.

Risk-Taking Leaders Step "Out Front" on Issues

- *"Texas does not provide insurance for males. It's a shame to be poor and unemployed in Texas – unless you're in prison."* –Pete Duarte, Chief Servant, Thomason Hospital, El Paso

- *"Ninety percent is excellent unless you are in the 10 percent without access to health care. I will not be satisfied with less than 100 percent."* –Ivan C.A. Walks, M.D., Chief Health Officer of the District of Columbia

- *"In this society, if you're an institution that is losing money, you are treated like a poor person. You are considered lazy and irresponsible."* –Patricia Gabow, M.D., CEO, Denver Health, in an interview with *Modern Healthcare* magazine

- *"It just makes good business sense. Health care professionals want to take care of those in need. An institutional commitment to the underserved makes recruitment and retention that much more successful."* –Charles T. Frock, President and CEO, FirstHealth of the Carolinas

- *"We had enough influence and enough of a track record that when we asked them to come to the table, they came. They trusted we would follow through. But Community Voices allowed us to frame the discussion."* –Jane Garcia, CEO, La Clinica de La Raza, Oakland

- *"The Community Voices approach encourages providers of health care and community leaders to think through ways to improve the health of the community through system changes rather than through narrow solutions which have limited impact on the overall health of the community."* –Allan J. Formicola, D.D.S., Columbia University School of Dental and Oral Surgery

Community Voices institutional leaders are not exactly shrinking violets when it comes to stating their opinions or pursuing objectives. Although they come from different parts of the country and lead distinct organizations, they share a clear vision of the benefits of collaboration through Community Voices approaches and an unflinching belief that doing the smart thing and the right thing are not incompatible. Whether representing health care organizations, academic institutions, health departments, or nonprofit organizations, each recognizes the connection between organizational mission and Community Voices objectives and draws heavily on the organization's reputation and relationships to marshal resources for collaborative targets.

These institutional leaders exhibit other common traits. They are not afraid to be out front on an issue, even an unpopular one. They are familiar with taking calculated risks. And they understand that institutions function within regulatory, public policy, and community environments – and are sensitive to the dynamics of all three. Community Voices project directors regard the guidance, credibility, and engagement of seasoned leaders as a pivotal factor in building collaboration. Many of these respected leaders were outspoken proponents of the needs of underserved community members and the responsibilities of institutions long before the initiative commenced.

Dr. Allan Formicola at Columbia University's School of Dental and Oral Surgery, for example, was making the case for dental schools to address oral health disparities years before the Community Voices initiative was envisioned. Community Voices made it possible for Dr. Formicola and his colleagues and community counterparts to work from a broader platform to engage public participation and attract additional partners to collaborative pursuits. Through his guidance, Columbia University's leadership in the Northern Manhattan Community Voices Collaborative encompasses the provision of health care; health professions education; and community-institutional partnerships combining research, practice, and community services.

Fueled by the community impact of Community Voices partnerships, Columbia is moving to formalize its role as convener and active partner. The creation of the Partnerships for Community Health Center has been approved by the Columbia board of trustees and will be housed on the University's Health Sciences campus. Northern Manhattan Community Voices Executive Director Sandra Harris explains, "The mission is to bring together faculty from the Health Sciences Campus and community groups and providers to assess community health needs, initiate and build partnerships, advocate on behalf of uninsured, and link education to the community at large." Dr. Formicola will assume leadership of the Center, and Community Voices will be one of many programs under its umbrella.

Other Community Voices projects have benefited from institutional leadership at this level and built upon the credibility and conviction of other seasoned leaders to engage community partners and spearhead successful collaboration.

• Jim Crouch, executive director of the California Rural Indian Health Board (CRIHB), traces CRIHB's roots to 1969. But Community Voices' Andy Anderson credits Crouch's 15 years as executive director with the "stability of leadership" essential to advancing the Turtle Health Plan. "His leadership and the maturity of CRIHB as an organization made such a bold move possible," Anderson believes.

• Sherry Hirota, CEO of Asian Health Services, and Jane Garcia, CEO of La Clinica de La Raza, drew on their many years of service and community clinic leadership first to attract partners to Oakland Community Voices collaboration and then to build a collaborative of safety net providers committed to a sustained community focus on expanding access. "Community Voices was the catalyst for a dialogue about systems," Hirota says. "It laid the way for creating a superstructure that has broadened the level of participation."

- Pete Duarte changed his Thomason Hospital CEO title to "Chief Servant" years ago. Born and raised in California, Duarte has been in El Paso since 1968 and an active supporter of building a community network of care for many years. "In my view, the hospital that keeps all of its resources within its walls is a thing of the past," Duarte states. He describes Community Voices as "the spark" to build collaboration and move toward integrated delivery of health care within the community.

- Patricia Gabow's reputation as both a respected physician and the capable administrator of a fully integrated health system with 3,000 employees has helped attract other leaders and build relationships for Denver Health Community Voices. Elizabeth Whitley mentions the policy board convened through Community Voices as an example of this credibility in action. "The number one person from each organization stepped forward to guide this process," she says.

- Through Community Voices, individual leaders are finding the mechanism to delve more deeply into challenges that threaten the viability and effectiveness of their safety net institutions. And in the process, the stature and profile of the organizations they lead are being raised – helping them attract capable collaborators.

Institutional Leaders Partner with Emerging Community Leaders

As part of the Community Voices initiative, academic institutions are demonstrating how their multi-faceted role as provider, educator, and partner can attract participation in broad-based collaboratives and leverage resources. Wayne Powell describes the University of New Mexico's boundary-crossing presence in his state as a prime example. "As the only medical school in New Mexico, the University of New Mexico (UNM) has a role as both provider and educator. It is also a pivotal part of the state safety net.

But through Community Voices partnerships, the connecting role of UNM has been elevated.

"UNM has helped develop common clinical protocols and practices. Through the Health Sciences Center's state-level connections, work undertaken through Community Voices to expand access to coverage through UNM Care is informing state-level policy discussions about financing strategies," Powell explains. "And as a partner, the University has helped bring together safety net providers as part of a consortium for the Community Access Program (CAP) grant. The more the University 'performs' as a partner, the more trusted it becomes."

> *"The more the University 'performs' as a partner, the more trusted it becomes."*
>
> —Wayne Powell,
> New Mexico

But Wayne Powell and other Community Voices leaders acknowledge that collaboration among institutions – working with and through established leaders who hold positions of authority within organizations – can only take you so far when it comes to community health. To underscore the point, he suggests a conversation with someone he describes as a "kindred spirit" – Steve Gonzales of Roswell, New Mexico.

"If good can come of it, you aren't going to stop me."
When Powell and Gonzales first met, Shared Solutions was exploring community health interests in the Roswell area. But Gonzales says he had been walking that path "in the barrio" for years prior. At the time, Gonzales remembers, "none of the dentists in Roswell wanted to work on Medicaid, Medicare, people with no money, little kids." He and a group of young people – members of all the different local gangs, in fact – were working together, silk-screening T-shirts in his garage and selling hot dogs at public functions to raise some money for dental care services. When Gonzales learned about the availability of an abandoned dental van in Portales – "and the local clinic said we could have it" – he took three grandsons, a battery charger, and his tools to where it sat 71 miles north of Roswell. "We must have been meant to have it," Gonzales recalls with a tinge of amazement, "because it started right up!"

After a harrowing drive back to Roswell ("No brakes, no registration, no insurance, and no radio!"), Gonzales and his neighborhood friends got started. He can list all of the local businesses and agencies that contributed funds or services to refurbish the van. "The county gave money to buy supplies. It needed new floors, new paint, everything." Gonzales handled the plumbing himself and before long, the van was operational and "things started falling into place," he says. "Eastern New Mexico University (ENMU) took over the van and three or four local dentists volunteered to work in it." Along with Jane Batson, director of the Health Education Division for ENMU in Roswell, Gonzales and his neighborhood collaborators began working closely with Community Voices. "Now in addition to the dental van," Gonzales says with satisfaction, "the clinic has two working dental rooms and two more being finished."

Gonzales says, "We did this 'the barrio way.'" But he also readily acknowledges the support Batson, Powell, and others have provided. "They have been our safety net. They didn't take credit and let us come up with ideas," he explains. "But they taught us how to do it." If anything, Gonzales downplays his role in raising community issues. "I'm not educated, didn't graduate," he is quick to say. "But I'm in it for the people. If good can come of it, you aren't going to stop me."

"I'm in it for the people. If good can come of it, you aren't going to stop me."

—Steve Gonzales, New Mexico

Gonzales traces his fervor and community involvement to 1993 when his son was shot and killed in the neighborhood. "That broke my bubble," he says quietly. "I came out into this different world when he got hurt. And I got up to fight." Powell, Batson, and many others credit Steve Gonzales's passion and persistence with more health options for Roswell people and better connections between institutions and community coalitions. "I was raised in the streets," says Gonzales. "Now the only difference is I don't fight with my hands. But I still let them have it. I don't hold back."

Steve Gonzales – with or without a formal position in any organization – is raising issues, engaging community resources, and building solid grounds for positive collaboration in Roswell. Powell and his colleagues believe grassroots leadership like Steve's – hands on, roll up your sleeves, "just do it" leadership – is invaluable, an essential element to improving community health and inspiring others to work for system change.

Identifying, Nurturing, Attracting Community Leadership

Finding and partnering with community leaders like Steve Gonzales has been one important thrust of every Community Voices project. Throughout the initiative, similar efforts are creating opportunities for capable community leaders to assume active roles in health decision making and pathways to nurture and sustain individuals and groups with the potential to lead. When Doak Bloss of Ingham Community Voices speaks of the tremendous importance of community leadership, relationship-building, and engagement, Ingham Health Plan Board Member Kathy Quick is one of the first people he mentions.

"Learning the Ins and Outs..."
Quick is one of 10 people serving on the Ingham Health Plan Corporation Board. As a community representative, Kathy Quick has been an Ingham Health Plan enrollee, and she says this dual role – board member and program recipient – helps her see both sides of coverage issues. She cites transportation as one of the difficulties faced by many community people and something she knows about firsthand. Quick takes three buses to get her son to appointments at a university clinic where, as she explains, "if we're ten minutes late, we have to reschedule." Accustomed to services "so far away it's unreal," Quick says recognizing the shortcomings of systems in place for poor people is the easy part of her board service.

"I understand why people don't want to put their kids on Medicaid even if they qualify. I didn't have my son on for two years. It's hard for some people to admit what they need for their families," she explains. "I hate walking into an office with that blue card. People treat you like you are lazy or an idiot!"

If identifying system barriers is the easy part of her role, Quick says "understanding the legal lingo" is one of the hard parts of board service. "When you get into a room with a bunch of suits, they talk that way all the time," she says matter-of-factly. "I need 'English for non-suits.' I need to know, but I don't always understand the way they explain it. It's not the way the rest of us talk." Quick adds, however, that "certain board members make you feel at ease. They'll say, 'Did you get that?' and encourage me to speak up if I have questions." And she is hardly the only board member with questions. The Ingham Health Plan's accounting firm provides sessions for all board members to ensure they understand the monthly reports. "Even retired doctors had a hard time reading the financials," she remembers. "We end up knowing everything whether we want to or not. Things I used to see only once a year at my church we see at every meeting."

Kathy Quick believes she has moved past the learning curve for active participation in the board process. But some challenges to participation are ongoing. "The time they meet, at 7:30 a.m., makes sense because they all have other jobs," she says. But transportation, arrangements for her son, and other logistical considerations require complicated planning in advance. Nevertheless, Quick's commitment to the Ingham Health Plan is a strong one. "Our prescription program is spreading to northern Michigan counties where it is greatly needed. I think the Ingham Health Plan for kids is going to take off too," she adds enthusiastically. "We tried to design something for people who don't have Medicaid." For Quick, connecting her experiences to health system processes and products is a tangible benefit.

"If you want things to change, you have to pipe up and say something."
—Kathy Quick, Ingham County

"My brain is growing," she says frankly. "I've needed to educate myself. Any average Joe would need to. Learning the ins and outs is the biggest thing for me." When asked what she thinks her fellow board members are learning through her participation, Quick says thoughtfully, "I think they understand a little bit more about stigma because I'm there. When you've got somebody hollering at you through the clinic window, 'Have you got your card?' so the whole waiting room can hear. It's about courtesy." Quick believes speaking up is her role. "If you want things to change, you have to pipe up and say something."

Community Leaders Setting the Course

Kathy Quick is making a significant contribution to Ingham Health Plan efforts. But she is emerging as one of a growing number of active, engaged community members gaining experience and information through Community Voices. Elsewhere in Ingham County, a neighborhood summit process led to the development of a local network of coalitions – coordinated health improvement teams that encompass neighborhood groups, churches, hospitals, university resources, and health department staff.

One collaborative effort through this process – the Data Democratization project – resulted in the creation of a website containing health and human services data from many public agencies. Online at <www.cacvoices.org>, community people can generate maps that track crime by neighborhood; produce charts detailing mortality or pregnancy rates; and identify local health, land, and water resources. Community Resource Navigators are trained as a part of this process, according to Ron Whitmore, coordinator of the Northwest Lansing Healthy Community Initiative. "It's a simple idea, but amazingly effective," he says. "Trained volunteer navigators – people in our neighborhood – help on a personal level so that others who lack access or are uncomfortable with technology can use it."

In North Carolina, FirstHealth Community Voices looks to employees to guide community connections. Employee Action Teams and community Compass Groups actively engage communities and link local leadership with health improvement efforts. "Our employees make up our community," says Lisa Hartsock. "As the largest employer in the region, our theory was that employees live in the neighborhoods we serve and others we still need to reach. Some of these employees are already working in their communities, but this gives them the opportunity to champion efforts they are directly interested in and provide additional resources." A Working Women's Closet project for welfare-to-work participants, health fairs and blood pressure screenings, refurbishing community centers, and a dozen other projects help to highlight the leadership of FirstHealth employees and connect the organization with broad community interests.

Art Gatling, a FirstHealth staffer who coordinates operating room supplies, says, "FirstHealth supports employees when they want to improve their communities and provides the resources to help them make a difference. Our communities are FirstHealth communities." Employee Action Teams laid the groundwork for Compass Groups – a formal FirstHealth strategy to make decisions about services and organization based on guidance from community members and providers in specific geographic regions. Hartsock points to this "decentralized planning" as an approach that "allows for more community input, quicker response rate to community interests, and greater creativity."

Creating a Resonant "We" Calling for Change
Within the context of Community Voices structures, "outsider"
positions can move to the forefront of community awareness as
those who call for community change, access new information,
and stand with others in the public arena. This dynamic of leadership – the force of calling others to action or gathering many voices into a single, resonant whole – is supporting Community Voices
project efforts in many venues and adding mass to the growing
catalog of data supporting fundamental change in health system
operations and financing.

"Who Speaks for the Uninsured?" is the headline of a *Miami
Herald* viewpoint. In the text that follows, Pedro Jose Greer, Jr., M.D.,
presses the issue of accountability as he describes unmet health
needs in Miami-Dade and the use of tax dollars intended for indigent
care within current systems. "Health care in Miami-Dade County is
in poor, probably critical, condition," he writes. "It is shocking and
unacceptable that 450,000 people are without health insurance.
That hundreds of thousands of our neighbors have no health coverage is just plain embarrassing." As a physician and adjunct faculty
member at the University of Miami School of Medicine, he recognizes the health consequences of these conditions.

As a member of the Community Voices Miami Oversight Team,
Greer knows where the money is going thanks to a funds flow
analysis completed by RAND. Without the data, his op-ed might
be a proverbial "cry in the wilderness." Ten years ago, Greer
admits ruefully, he served on an indigent care task force, and the
issues raised at that time still persist. But he sees some hope in the
wake of the RAND report and Community Voices collaboration
around access and coverage for uninsured and underserved. "Now
people realize that we have spent $1 billion in tax dollars – money
earmarked for indigent care from the half-penny surtax – and
nothing has changed. The next step is the Mayor's Task Force."
With the information at hand and "everybody at the table," Greer
says he hopes to see greater accountability and system change.

RAND's Catherine Jackson says she and her colleagues are
"gratified" by the practical application of report data as part of the
Community Voices process. "Our work on *Hospital Care for the
Uninsured in Miami-Dade County: Hospital Finance and Patient
Travel Patterns* has generated discussion about how care for the
uninsured is financed in the county and where the uninsured

receive care," she notes. "When we started this project three years ago, the conventional wisdom was that the half-penny sales tax was levied to provide funds for indigent care. Through the course of our research, we learned that this was not the case." The discussion generated, as a result, indicates that the community needs to clarify its intent and address public accountability issues, she believes – a necessary part of the change process. "It is through this type of public dialogue that local policy can change," Jackson suggests, "and we are heartened to see it occur."

> "We want to put health issues high on the public agenda."
>
> —Vincent DeMarco, Baltimore

Through another Community Voices project, the rallying cry for change comes from a statewide grassroots coalition attracting public attention and gaining momentum. At the lead is Dr. Peter Beilenson, Baltimore city health commissioner, who is also president of the Maryland Citizens' Health Initiative. With 2,200 organizations in its membership, including labor organizations and trade groups, the League of Women Voters, faith organizations, nonprofits, and many others, Executive Director Vincent DeMarco says, "We'll be in the *Guinness Book of World Records* one of these days." But that's not the sort of recognition the coalition is seeking. "We want to put health issues high on the public agenda," DeMarco explains.

The organization's "Health Care for All" campaign has evolved into a tangible plan to offer universal health coverage to the state's uninsured children and adults. Material available at the organization's website, <www.healthcareforall.com>, provides ample information to help community people understand the proposed plan, how it would be financed, and why it is necessary. "We're all about collaboration," says DeMarco. "It's the key to what we offer." The collaboration is empowering participating organizations and mainstreaming an issue that attracts leadership from health, human services, education, and labor.

The Community Voices partnership in Baltimore, was an early supporter of the Maryland Citizen's Health Initiative. Funds contributed in the campaign's infancy were leveraged into a tenfold financial commitment from other funders, including the Annie E. Casey Foundation. And the coalition's plan is attracting media attention in nearby Washington, D.C., and elsewhere. In an interview with the *Washington Post*, Beilenson commented that after eight years as city health commissioner "it became obvious that the system was so broken that incremental change would not make a difference." By building a strong, focused coalition to raise awareness and explore options, Beilenson and Maryland Citizens' Health Initiative partners are helping to craft "an economically and politically viable" approach to secure high-quality, affordable health care for all of Maryland's uninsured.

Partnerships Bridge Interests through Common Targets

Community Voices brokers partnerships to create formal ways to "stand together" on issues, reduce duplication of effort and increase coordination, broaden the base of support for an activity or endeavor, and attract additional resources. Partnerships reflect the necessary self-interest of organizational participants in a positive and practical way. Acting as convener, collaborator, *and* partner, Community Voices is called to recognize the need for safety net organizations to relate coalition activities and investments to its core missions. The agreements that frame partnerships provide an opportunity for discussion of these needs and explore ways to work together that will satisfy all partners.

Partnerships often make it possible for organizations to take the lead on particular issues – and share the limelight – as part of a larger strategy for building a stronger overall safety net for communities. Partnerships negotiated with participants' basic interests acknowledged and respected encourage organizations and institutions to come together across turf lines and competing markets. Community Voices project directors point to healthy, working partnerships as one indicator of sustainability for future efforts. And some Community Voices projects pursue partnerships as a primary organizing strategy to accomplish objectives.

"We practice what we preach . . ."
The West Virginia Community Voices Partnership works with and through lead partners – assisting these nonprofit organizations and the community collaborative efforts they support to expand access to health care, raise oral health issues, and promote community

engagement. Paul Gilmer, senior vice president for LifeBridge, Inc., and an active West Virginia Community Voices Partnership participant, says the "coordinating and collaborating" in process is just how "we practice what we preach." Based on his organization's recent transitions, Gilmer is in a good position to "preach."

When Community Voices began, Gilmer was head of the Community Council of Kanawha Valley – an organization that merged with United Way of Kanawha Valley, in part, as a result of Community Voices collaboration. "There was talk about the merger for a long time," Gilmer recalls. "But turf issues were somehow never resolved." So Community Council and United Way found themselves "sitting in the same meetings, doing fundraising in the community, running programs," Gilmer says. "The more we came together to facilitate a community dialogue through Community Voices, we said, 'Why not pare this thing down and put it together?'"

> "If you wait until the community is in crisis mode, you spend all your resources being reactive."
>
> —Paul Gilmer,
> West Virginia

The new organization pooled resources and reorganized to keep the same community-focused goals but work more efficiently. "LifeBridge has four divisions encompassing the services, programming, and development functions our two organizations handled before." The difference, Gilmer believes, is in the fourth division – one focused on planning, research, and allocation of resources according to needs. Gilmer indicates that the new division has the potential to raise issues and addresses systemic problems in a way previous programming could not. "If you wait until the community is in crisis mode, you spend all your resources being reactive," he says. "By assessing community needs and allocating resources based on that information, we can anticipate and address problems before they create a crisis."

Nancy Tolliver of the West Virginia Community Voices Partnership notes, "Community Voices served as both model and partner in the process of negotiating a successful merger between the United Way of Kanawha Valley and Community Council of Kanawha Valley." The new hybrid organization remains a strong partner for the many Community Voices efforts.

In addition to regional partnerships, West Virginia Community Voices worked with key partners and the state Bureau for Public Health to foster the development of a Minority Health Program.

Given the state's small proportion of minority residents (4 percent), the health disparities that exist – especially in urban areas – often are minimized. Savolia Spottswood, director of the Minority Health Program, says that is changing thanks to the partnership between Community Voices and the Bureau for Public Health. "The state of West Virginia has truly turned the first corner in building capacity for minority health issues to be addressed. Minority health issues are now on the radar screen of access to quality health services' agenda; the Partnership with African American Churches has staff support; and additional funding has been obtained for initiatives seeking to positively impact the health of minorities," she explains. "Community Voices has been the catalyst for many changes from which minority populations have benefited – and will continue to benefit."

Partnership Strategies Join Competitors, Foster Coordination

Renate Pore, past director of the West Virginia Community Voices Partnership and active participant in the process at multiple levels, believes that the partnership strategy is instructive for nonprofits, state agencies, philanthropies, and health organizations. "We have learned that bringing people together who have an interest in an issue," Pore reflects, "and providing them with small amounts of money that they can leverage to other funders has allowed us to do a lot of things that we would otherwise not have been able to do without this kind of coordination through Community Voices." Partnership experiences in other Community Voices communities are bearing out her observation.

The partnership strategy is instructive for nonprofits, state agencies, philanthropies, and health organizations.

• The Community Voices Collaborative of the District of Columbia is situated within the D.C. Department of Health and Program Manager Judith Johnson sees evidence that the close proximity is promoting formal connections and informal linkages within and outside of the Department. "Positioning the Community Voices Collaborative in the Department of Health has enabled a more intimate working relationship with the entity responsible for managing and administering the city's public health care system," Johnson notes. "Like many health departments across the nation, the Department has begun the process of shifting its focus from the delivery of direct services toward health assessment, policy development, and quality assurance." She believes that the Collaborative's community-focused organization and committee structure fosters partnerships between health providers, community organizations, and Department of Health administrations. For instance, funding for the Consumer Health Access Teams (CHAT) outreach efforts joins Community Voices with the Department's Maternal and Child Health Administration and the Safety Net Administration.

- Partnerships undertaken through the Voices of Detroit Initiative (VODI) are mindful of the practical considerations of partnering with competitors and related trust issues. "Although our partners share the VODI vision to improve access to health care services and the health status of city of Detroit residents, we developed written principles for how principal partners will work together on the development of an Integrated Delivery System," VODI's Lucille Smith explains. "The partnership is stronger as a result and, in the end, our shared vision of improved access to care for the uninsured is far more important than any differences." Through the VODI Community Access Program (CAP) grant, partners have leveraged resources to continue to explore models for providing care to meet the service needs of Detroit's most vulnerable.

A Responsive Infrastructure of Relationships

Community Voices project directors indicate that interpersonal connections, leadership, and partnerships are all part of an infrastructure of relationships they see as essential to program sustainability and the expansion of collaborative efforts. And, although safety net providers continue to function within the larger health care marketplace, some important dynamics are beginning to change at the community and regional levels.

Years of working shoulder to shoulder to hammer out new coverage options and care management approaches are giving Community Voices participants the experiences they need to regard traditional competitors as trustworthy allies. In many cities and states, providers and consumers are sitting down with county and state agency officials to determine how best to use scarce resources to reach underserved people. Tools developed to assist health systems track enrollment and utilization are in use in nonprofits and public agencies. Data and analysis from expanded programming and coverage are being shared across communities, regionally, and with state and federal agencies as evidence that systems are capable of positive change in response to – and in collaboration with – communities.

Community Voices project directors increasingly describe these connections as adaptive, cohesive, and nimble – capable of reacting quickly and capably to changes in the environment and opportunities for their communities. The stronger the bonds between collaborative partners, the more storms weathered and problems solved, the greater the capacity to respond to new situations and keep moving toward common goals.

The discussion begun at a Community Voices meeting may be continued at a state-level task force session or a medical society gathering.

For the people guiding Community Voices projects, this web of connections has become both interpersonal and professional. The "face time" in meetings is making it easier to pick up the phone with a question or pass along some useful nugget of information to a colleague across town. The casual conversations about kids or sports or family plans are uncovering commonalities that stay with participants long after meetings conclude. The discussion begun at a Community Voices meeting may be continued at a state-level task force session or a medical society gathering. As participants move to other organizations or assume new roles within institutions, some bonds are stretching and new links being established. Since Community Voices connections are based on firsthand experiences, they are reshaping people, their perceptions, and relationships.

And, thanks to connections established and strengthened through Community Voices networking across projects, these changes are not taking place in a void. Risk-taking leaders need a peer group. Hard-won insights and data from experiences in one community may serve to guide or galvanize partners working in another. Community Voices networking meetings and the relationships that form as a result are creating a cadre of leaders and a committed corps of change agents to assist and support colleagues across time and distance.

"Ready to be 'real partners' with government ..."
Viewed as a whole, the vibrancy of the leadership, partnerships, and relationships driving Community Voices programming seems to have its roots in the pent-up frustrations of uninsured people, safety net providers, nonprofit directors, and many other health system stakeholders. By creating a mechanism to approach this troubling problem from a fresh angle, and through the process of investing resources and producing tangible results, Community Voices is giving rise to hopeful inclinations among participants. And that hope is inspiring others. Community Voices partners do not claim to have remade their community safety nets or solved the puzzle of how to provide health care for all given marketplace constraints, but they are figuring out how to do more and do better. They are learning, and they recognize the value of what they are accomplishing on a larger scale.

Renate Pore believes the most enduring lesson from Community Voices connections may lie in understanding what the model demonstrates about communities and providers as potential partners. "Communities and providers are ready to be 'real partners' with government to solve this problem," she states. "They want to be responsible and responsive; they do see things in a system perspective. Now government needs to reach out to communities and become partners. Government needs to solve the financing piece; communities will figure out how to provide good care and save dollars." Community Voices participants are showing the way.

Chapter 8:
Timely Practice and Policy Lessons from Community Voices

In the months and years since the Community Voices initiative was conceived and begun, the world around health and human service systems in the United States has changed more than a little. While the policies and practices that created strain on safety net systems in the late 1990s have continued, the economy first peaked, then plummeted, and now is beginning its rebound. More importantly, the events of September 11th, the anthrax crises that followed, and the nation's military action in Afghanistan changed the country's priorities and ushered in an era of less-than-certain homeland security as we confronted unsuspected vulnerability within our boundaries.

It would be fair to ask, in the wake of so much change, if lessons from the Community Voices initiative are still relevant. With the federal government necessarily giving its attention to national security and world affairs, and state and county entities managing budget issues and new demands for homeland security, is this a reasonable time to "tinker" with vital health care systems and raise awareness of shortcomings? Wouldn't it be better to save these issues for another, more peaceful, less complicated time?

Community Voices partners would be the first to acknowledge that their communities, like communities across the nation, have been stunned, shaken, and deeply sobered by recent events. Initiative partners in Northern Manhattan and Washington, D.C., where the attacks of September 11th scarred both the landscape and the local psyche with unspeakable loss, are all too mindful of the division between "then" and "now." In Detroit, Michigan; Alameda County, California; El Paso, Texas; and Miami, Florida – all communities with large immigrant populations whose boundaries abut international borders or waters – the differences in the environment and the political climate cannot be ignored.

Yet all say that, even as world conflicts and security issues absorb attention and resources, the needs at the community level in most U.S. cities and towns persist. Emergency rooms remain crowded; even more people work at low-wage jobs; and the demands on safety net systems by the poor, the uninsured, and the vulnerable continue unabated. In fact, demands are on the rise as these same safety net institutions – hospitals, public health departments, clinics, and health centers – are recognized as pivotal pressure points in a post-September 11th United States. Caring for the most vulnerable, they constitute a first line of defense against bioterrorism with the potential to identify, contain, and monitor possible threats to our health and safety.

Safety net institutions constitute a first line of defense against bioterrorism.

Added to this, the shadow issues that lurked in the health system background in 1998 seem more visible among the general population today. More low-income and contract workers without health coverage; significant gaps in oral and mental health services for poor people; men and women newly-released from prison without access to health care or coverage; precious few primary care access points for undocumented immigrants, single men, older women, people of color, rural residents – these conditions continue to trouble communities, press health systems, and place disproportionate burdens on poor people. Despite the uplifting solidarity and generous impulses prompted by the events of September 11th, nothing of substance is altered in low-income communities or within the safety net systems providing their care.

Balancing Costs and Care

Actually, the costs of health care and coverage sharply increased as 2001 came to a close even as reimbursement levels for public programs, such as Medicare, declined. Now, more doctors are saying they cannot afford to take new Medicare patients and stay afloat – a position familiar to people depending on Medicaid coverage for access to care. As a result, a part of the safety net once considered sturdy has become more fragile, and health systems, especially the safety net systems that function as providers of last resort in low-income communities, find themselves confronting pressure from yet another flank.

As precious and essential as most people believe good health to be, the basics of health care are moving out of reach for growing numbers of community members with limited resources – try as they might to balance the tremendous costs of health care services with competing demands for housing, food, transportation, and family care. And cost is only one dimension of this dilemma, to be sure. Barriers to accessing care in current systems – obstacles rooted in language and cultural differences, distance, stigma, and provider shortages, for instance – represent another layer. And the complexities embedded in disjointed payment streams and practice parameters obstruct the pathway for many people *with* resources, let alone those without.

Every day, individuals without access to coverage or health care make difficult choices in light of these conditions. Administrators in the health departments and hospitals they turn to face the same issues in one form or another. And as they do, institutional and public policymakers, decision makers in philanthropic and nonprofit organizations, and community leaders consider related decisions about how to allocate resources. To the extent that all of these people wonder how to make sense of health care and health care systems in this environment, lessons from Community Voices projects are not only relevant, but timely and important.

The marketplace orientation of the system as a whole is squeezing out more people as costs rise.

The premise of the Community Voices initiative, after all, is that the health system does not work for everybody. Unfortunately, the accuracy of that premise becomes daily more apparent in most communities. The marketplace orientation of the system as a whole is squeezing out more people as costs rise. The inherent fragmentation that separates funding for and access to physical, oral, mental, and behavioral health care continues to frustrate both consumers and providers who must wrestle with its baffling complexities. The striking health disparities present in most communities – between people of color and white Americans, immigrants and citizens, those with health coverage and those without it, rich and poor – seem fixed and intractable. And the lack of adequate coverage and comprehensive care for people from childhood through adulthood all but ensures that Social Security, Medicare, and Medicaid will continue to bear the tremendous fiscal burden of caring for very sick elderly.

Since September 11th, new demands on limited public health resources and an estimated combined $40 billion deficit looming for state governments in 2002 mean that the programs in place (especially Children's Health Insurance Program and Medicaid)

147

face significant cuts in funding in the near term. With no foreseeable change in demographic trends related to growing numbers of people of color, immigrant families, ex-offenders, older women, and others largely left out of the health care marketplace, Community Voices models for reorienting local health services delivery, practice, and financing are needed now more than ever.

Local Solutions, National Relevance

Because the 13 Community Voices projects function as learning laboratories, the community-driven changes undertaken by local, regional, and state-level partners have been developed with a watchful eye on national issues. Some of the products of their partnership endeavors have been the subject of previous chapters – examples of community-specific approaches to expanding access to care and coverage for uninsured and underserved people. As Community Voices participants refine local solutions and expand efforts piloted through the initiative, they continue to gather data, measure results, and share information with federal policymakers, colleagues in professional organizations and advocacy groups, and across communities of interest. But they also strive to distill the essential elements of the Community Voices process – both to apply lessons to other streams of work and understand what makes some approaches unqualified "hits" and others disappointing "misses."

Community Voices partners have participated in regular interviews, phone conferences, and networking sessions over the past few years, discussing and debating the best advice to pass along to others seeking to strengthen safety net systems by reorienting approaches to caring for the underserved. Part of the drive to understand and explain both products and processes of this initiative is rooted in experience. Community Voices participants recognize that what they have to share is not a simple recipe ("Take two parts leadership, three healthy partnerships, and a pinch of capital ..."). Explaining *how* something occurred, *what* is changing, and *why* it is important – these are the challenges for Community Voices participants as they try to weave their individual project experiences into a practical path for others. At the outset of Community Voices, they faced uncertain territory with no proven guide. Three years later, Community Voices projects have models in place that can serve to guide other communities with the will to address health disparities by expanding access. They recognize that their collective message has particular relevance for key audiences – institutional and public policymakers, decision makers in philanthropic organizations, and program directors and community leaders – and they want it heard loud and clear.

To that end, Community Voices program leaders and participants recommend the following ways of working as lessons from their collaborative efforts of three years. Acknowledging that each community is distinct – and its make up, interests, resources, and state of readiness different from every other community – Community Voices participants respectfully submit these promising approaches as worthy of consideration for future investment. These are the approaches they have come to trust – the ones they believe have been crucial to the development of viable products and enduring connections to bolster ongoing efforts. Taken together, Community Voices program leaders believe these straightforward dictums help explain the how, what, and why of their progress to date.

Change the question and listen intently to answers.

"We all think health care should change – just not us. But the longer we take, the more people suffer. We're making a good living. It's not about us." –Pedro Jose Greer, Jr., M.D., Miami

What is health? What do you value about health and health care? What gets in the way of you and your family maintaining health? What can we – or should we as a community – do about it? Open-ended questions like these are not the usual points of departure for health programs, according to Community Voices participants. Traditionally, health system experts (health care providers, health departments, academic health systems) identify a community health issue, assess local needs and system resources, craft a programmatic solution, and seek to implement it in the target neighborhood or region. Community Voices, on the other hand, started from the premise that engagement and broad-based participation were essential to reaching and learning from underserved health care consumers. To initiate conversations they hoped would spark a dialogue, Community Voices lead partners approached a variety of health system stakeholders with atypical questions – and kept asking them in interviews, forums, focus groups, and other venues. The result of posing broad questions and listening – really listening – to the answers has taken program efforts in directions many would not have envisioned. Change the question, Community Voices program leaders say, and you change the way you approach issues, direct resources, and seek solutions.

This question-and-answer cycle has been one of the strengths of the Community Voices process, participants believe. Because changing the questions you ask – and widening the circle of those you seek answers from – can reshape staid approaches and generate fundamentally different solutions. In Ingham County responses, the implications of a single question, "What is health?" guided development of a countywide action plan, expanded oral health services, launched a coverage program for 13,000 low-income community people, increased participation in community health decision making, and established a mechanism for accountability to assess progress toward targets.

"Listening is key to a consumer-driven process."

—Hakim Farrakhan, Baltimore

The dialogue process that grew from that single question "changed the environment," Ingham County Health Officer Bruce Bragg insists. In Baltimore, Hakim Farrakhan of Bon Secours Baltimore Health System credits a similar Community Voices strategy with investments in an innovative service delivery model.

Community answers to broad questions in Baltimore's Sandtown-Winchester neighborhood guided the development of the nation's first Men's Health Center. "Is men's health a public health issue? Yes. Absolutely," Farrakhan says. But health systems alone might not have come up with that focus, he admits. "Listening is key to a consumer-driven process." Virtually every Community Voices project has started with an out-of-the-box question and found ways to listen intently to the answers provided by uninsured community members, safety net providers, human service organizations, community and faith leaders, state administrators, business people, and many other stakeholders. Energy dedicated to this process dimension of the Community Voices model has been essential to development of tangible products and strategies for expanding access to care and coverage for underserved community members.

Reinvent the wheel.

"Get rid of the term 'less fortunate.' Erase the labels and categories. Dump the idea that only 'the leaders' or providers know what's best."
–Chuck Steinberg, President, Ingham Health Plan Corporation Board

Community Voices program leaders from institutions and communities are practical people. And like most practical people, they are interested in making the best use of resources and avoiding duplication of efforts. But they also recognize that sometimes you have to start from scratch to reorient entrenched systems and create something new. So they're willing to ignore conventional wisdom and start over, if that's what it will take to see results. Because where conventional wisdom says, "Be wary of competitors. There are only so many pieces of the pie to go around. More for them means less for me," Community Voices counters with "Collaborate. Form partnerships. We can do more together." While traditional management approaches advise, "Get the power people in a room and 'cut to the chase,'" Community Voices advocates, "Throw a wide net, engage all stakeholders, and keep the forum open." Community Voices leaders recognize that conventional wisdom may constitute a form of avoidance or resistance to change. And their ultimate goal is making sense of health care systems – creating organized systems of care that do a better job of improving community health. So they try approaches that seem to fly in the face of convention, reasoning that "the way things have always been done" created the fragmented, costly systems in place.

The ultimate goal is creating organized systems of care that do a better job of improving community health.

All systems resist change. Those with power are reluctant to share it. At some level, a natural inertia makes it easier to go with the prevailing "flow" than swim upstream. But Community Voices programs and conceptual approaches have done just that in many instances – taken the best from existing practices and jettisoned the rest in favor of something that makes more sense. The New Mexico health commons concept pools resources across physical, mental, oral, and behavioral health to address the primary health care and human service needs of local uninsured and underserved. Alameda County's Family Care program for low-income uninsured creates seamless coverage and care for previously uninsured families regardless of immigration status. The California Rural Indian Health Board's Turtle Health Plan places the locus of control for financing, service design, data collection, and management of health coverage and care in the hands of Indian tribes and their leaders. These are not incremental changes, but fundamental reorientations of "the way things have always been done." Yet Community Voices programs make more sense for the communities they serve, make better use of available resources, and hold more promise for improving community health over the long term. In many respects, they seek to "reinvent the wheel," if the wheel does not serve the community's interests, needs, and desires. Community Voices leaders say that, sometimes, reinventing the wheel is the wisest course of all.

Don't stand alone. Collaborate to mainstream issues and products.

"In my experience, Community Voices has moderated the competition between health care systems, hospitals, and other providers resulting in a collaborative effort for the provision of services and benefits to uninsured and underserved." –John B. Waller, Jr., Senior Vice President, Detroit Medical Center

Describing successful, effective Community Voices programs and activities requires long lists of participants – including lead partners, collaborative groups, and the names of many diverse institutions and organizations. Presenting, more or less, the opposite profile of those lean, flat organizational models favored by marketplace ideology, Community Voices clusters and groupings could seem almost cumbersome by comparison. But participants insist that the many connections formed through Community Voices are, in fact, the secret to program successes. By establishing neutral forums and "taking all comers," Community Voices projects have worked hard to diffuse wedge tactics and minimize turf battles. Even as products and activities have shown results – thereby attracting greater involvement from more aloof partners and sometimes the support of former critics – Community Voices program leaders say their collaboratives strive to remain open; to add people; to create a bigger, more inclusive umbrella that enjoins ever more participants. Products developed in one health system or department are linked to funding and activities across departments, health systems, and partner organizations. This is strategic, Community Voices program leaders insist, and key to long-term sustainability. Collaboration is a potent strategy for connecting streams of thinking and working to more organizations and communities of interest. Neutral forums can engage a wider circle of stakeholders in problem solving, Community Voices participants know – forums that spark dialogue and fuel the development of solutions that encompass health programs, health care education and practice, and institutional and public policy discussions.

Collaboration makes it possible to instigate dialogue around complex issues rather than debate. Standing with other safety net institutions and consumers is making it possible for Community Voices collaboratives to raise the profile of issues – oral health, mental health, universal coverage, health system practices, and prudent use of resources – as they foster broad-based conversations and support the development of communitywide responses. Collaboration through Community Voices partners in Miami is helping the community address troubling health disparities and funding streams that constrain the current use of resources. In Northern Manhattan, Community Voices participants – consumers, providers, agency decision makers, academic health systems – have come together to identify the range of community issues at play in unmet mental health needs. As a result, they are joined in the development of solutions and strategies as well, and using the products of their collective work to draw others into the process. Through the Maryland Citizens' Health Initiative, leaders from public health, health systems, labor, advocacy groups, and other agencies are bringing their collective energies to bear on the problem of uninsured in their state. They are raising the profile of health as an issue and building a base of support for the development of solutions. This type of political collaboration is animating Community Voices programming, advocacy, and sustainability as participants explore opportunities for "standing together" around common issues and promising products.

Collaboration is animating Community Voices programming, advocacy, and sustainability.

Generate data, but don't wait to act.

"We didn't wait for proof that this product would fill a gap for low-income families. Based on our focus groups, we just decided to plunge in. In this arena, if you wait around, you have no innovation. There is no scientific, perfectly quantified data – and there will always be a million reasons not to do this. Sometimes you have to take a risk to make something happen." –Irene Ibarra, CEO, Alameda Alliance for Care, California

Community Voices projects are learning laboratories, framing questions and seeking answers for the benefit of their communities as well as others who can learn from their collective efforts. So they have a keen interest in generating credible evidence as they pursue project targets – data to explain and support the conclusions they draw from specific investments of time, personnel, and resources. Yet they recognize that waiting for data can be an excuse *not* to take action. As collaborators in past task forces and other initiatives, Community Voices partners knew that the "we need to do a study" direction often was more than capable of forestalling the development of programmatic solutions to pressing community problems. Information is essential to making a case for the investment of scarce resources, of course, and safety net organizations are perennially short of resources. But partners reasoned that the need for data to support decisions must be balanced with the benefits to be gained by taking action. As learning laboratories, Community Voices projects have been able to straddle these two competing imperatives. With dedicated resources from initiative funding, they have possessed both the means and the impetus for doing *first* and learning in the process. And the freedom to follow the preliminary advice from community stakeholders – to go ahead and try something that might or might not succeed and gain valuable experience in the doing – has been liberating, according to Community Voices program leaders.

By erring on the side of action, Community Voices has extended the learning curve for community safety net systems. In some cases, projects are piloting approaches – testing on a small scale a programmatic direction or group of activities that otherwise might not be tried. Elsewhere, Community Voices partners are launching full-scale operations to reorient community systems and gain valuable experience in the process. In Denver, Community Voices collaboration is linking community outreach workers with expanded and redesigned enrollment activities connecting public health, hospitals, and community organizations. As uninsured and underserved people are drawn into care and coverage systems, many become part of case management programs developed to coordinate care, link patients to additional resources, and provide the needed support to improve health outcomes and manage chronic conditions. Denver Health Community Voices and its partners are learning from this process, to be sure, but the activities improving care for the most vulnerable are making that learning possible. In the same way, the New Mexico Shared Solutions dental program has grown exponentially in a very short period of time. Unmet community needs and dental personnel shortages statewide have demanded rapid growth, Shared Solutions partners say. Is the program meeting all existing needs? Absolutely not, they admit. But the dental program is "plunging in" anyway – documenting the extent of practice and resource issues, relating what is being learned to institutional and public policy discussions, and providing much-needed care in the process. Data will come from these related efforts as programming continues. But in the meantime, Community Voices activities are expanding access to health care and demonstrating the utility of implementing programs and learning from them simultaneously. With community will and collaborative support, program leaders say, you can do both.

Navigate systems; redirect resources.

"Recognize the obvious: You already ARE taking care of everyone. Step up, declare your commitment, and develop an organized way to deliver care in a cost-effective way." –Charles T. Frock, President and CEO, FirstHealth of the Carolinas

This rebuttal to the predictable refrain, "We can't take care of *everyone!*" describes a can-do attitude that Community Voices participants say has been galvanizing. Instead of explaining why change is not possible or how past efforts failed, Community Voices projects "just do it," as program leaders like to say. Their jumping off point is an alternate premise – that it *is* possible to create rational systems of care that work for both safety net providers and vulnerable populations. With time, resources, and a framework that supports connections, traditional competitors can collaborate. Consumers can partner with providers to guide the development of viable coverage and care options. Resources can be identified and leveraged to expand access to health coverage and care for uninsured and underserved. And people who typically depend on emergency rooms for services can be drawn into systems of primary care and prevention. Wishing alone doesn't make it so, program leaders emphasize. To accomplish previously unimagined shifts in local health delivery practices, Community Voices projects navigate health and human service systems and redirect resources to reorient health activities, the locus of programming, funding streams, and perceptions about essential personnel. Based on successful programs and savvy partnerships now up and running at Community Voices sites, participants can point to any number of changes as indicators that their beliefs about what is possible were well-founded.

Health systems that make sense from the community perspective look very different from traditional health care models.

Health systems that make sense from the community perspective may look very different from traditional health care models, Community Voices participants have learned. As Voices of Detroit Initiative (VODI) partners know, health access points in these reoriented systems may be many and far outside of hospital walls. Health outreach workers and community promotoras are often at the center of these reoriented systems, as they are in El Paso and the District of Columbia – helping those on the margins of traditional health system markets to acquire needed skills to improve health and the resources to access care. Health systems, public health, and other institutions may come together to draw people from underserved communities into health professions career paths, as they have in Denver and Northern Manhattan. Such collaborations ensure a pipeline of community leadership and providers with the potential to reflect not only the diversity, but the perspectives of vulnerable populations. Health services delivery systems that generally compete in the marketplace pool resources to create efficient, seamless streams of care and coverage for previously uninsured community members, like Alameda

County's model. The working definitions of health and health care in Community Voices models (like those in New Mexico, Ingham County, and other project sites) encompass an array of services community people may need to attain health – often including dental care, mental and behavioral health services, job training, and/or affordable housing. Funding for needed services – language access, enrollment support, care coordination, transportation – is diverted from other cost centers and leveraging of new funds ensures that health improves as a result of community investments. Under existing practice and policy parameters, these systems are not simple, but they do make more sense, according to Community Voices participants. And they do illustrate the utility of navigating systems and redirecting resources to expand access to coverage and care.

Infuse passion with pragmatism.

"The number one risk to health is apathy." –Ivan C.A. Walks, M.D., Chief Health Officer of the District of Columbia

To say that Community Voices program leaders as a group are passionate about their work would be an understatement, at the very least. By and large, they are determined to improve health access for people in their communities – uninsured, people of color, single men, older women, immigrants, low-income families, rural residents – any and all of those who find themselves excluded from the health care marketplace by income or circumstance. They recognize the community impact of health disparities rooted in poverty, racism, and the policies that relegate the least powerful to a fragmented and inadequate second tier of health care under current systems. They chafe as those *with* health resources easily access MRIs and mammograms for diagnosis or prevention, prescription drugs for depression or other mental health needs, and cosmetic as well as preventative dental care while those *without* cut blood pressure pills in half or go without medication, lose teeth, and depend on periodic acute illnesses to bring them within range of much-needed health care

Community Voices program leaders see issues in human terms and use every tool to reshape systems.

services. Community Voices program leaders see these issues in very human terms and use every tool within reach to reshape systems to better address community needs.

Yet their passion is tempered by a pragmatism that makes it possible to attract partners with quite different perspectives. For as fervently as some Community Voices participants decry the health access and health outcome discrepancies between rich and poor, immigrant and native born, white and African American and Hispanic, urban and rural, many others are more mindful of the constant struggle to balance the budgets of safety net institutions and stop the cash flow draining their organizations. Community Voices program leaders understand that stakeholders from public health agencies, county and state governments, hospitals, and other institutions must consider their own survival needs first. And if the interests and insights of consumers and underserved community members are vital to the Community Voices process, so also are the perspectives and difficult positions of local and state-level health systems, agencies, and organizations. Community Voices program leaders believe the success of project efforts thus far can be traced to this combination of passion and pragmatism. Such fusion makes it possible for California Rural Indian Health Board (CRIHB) leaders to relate Turtle Health Plan to the needs and practical interests of tribal leaders, Indian clinic providers, and state officials at the California Department of Health Services. The same dynamic impels the District of Columbia Community Voices Collaborative to create mechanisms for consumer voices as well as Health Department administrations, local providers, academic institutions, and neighborhood agencies to work together. In virtually every Community Voices project site, the understandable zeal to meet the needs of underserved is tethered to dollar-and-cents strategies to strengthen safety net providers and community systems of care. Community Voices program leaders note that the data and collaborative experience produced through project efforts is laying the groundwork for long-term sustainability and expanded cooperation.

Connect the dots.

"Community Voices communities and health care providers are working together to take responsibility for the health of their populations.

But they cannot do it on their own." —Renate Pore, West Virginia Governor's Council on Children and Families

Programming, practice, and policy education are the dots Community Voices participants are seeking to align. But the opportunity to do so is a new one for many participants. "We have always worked on program issues," says Jane Garcia in describing both La Clinica de La Raza and Asian Health Services' traditional role. "Community Voices gave us the opportunity to inform policy issues and be creative. That has been a critical piece." Garcia's analysis is echoed across Community Voices projects. Program leaders believe that their learning-laboratory function heightened awareness of the implications of local efforts and created the expectation for dissemination beyond their immediate communities of interest. They also see ways it has shaped their choice of partners, strategic approaches, and investments. Knowing that local or regional Community Voices activities carry implications in the broader national context surrounding health issues, individual projects have taken pains to draw health system stakeholders outside of their communities into project efforts. Across the initiative, Community Voices networking meetings, website content, reports, and surveys have helped program leaders bring their collective experiences and communities' insights to bear on national discussions.

Local or regional Community Voices activities carry implications in the broader national context.

By relating programming experiences to the regulatory parameters that shape practice patterns and funding streams, Community Voices project experiences even now are educating administrators at the state level and identifying barriers to improving community health. In North Carolina, FirstHealth Community Voices efforts to expand access to oral health care for children have highlighted fluoride varnish and sealant practice guidelines. Dr. Sharon Harrell, director of the program, explains: "Providing care to children on a daily basis enables us to see firsthand which practice changes would best improve the health of our target population. Being on the front line in providing care also gives us the insight to identify policy revisions which reduce the barriers to access to care for the underserved." West Virginia Community

Voices Partnerships are linking outreach and enrollment in existing coverage programs with state-level discussions. In fact, each and every Community Voices project is engaged in policy education and informing discussions related to individual project targets. Although initially, some Community Voices partners may have been less familiar with this role, all readily acknowledge, at the initiative's halfway mark, that the emphasis on relating programs to practice and regulatory parameters – and bringing project experiences to policy discussions at the state and federal levels – has been an important strategy for strengthening the community safety net, leveraging resources, and raising the profile of issues critical to improving community health.

Take the time to build something better.

"Lessons learned include that access to health insurance does not mean that your clients will present for health care. In other words, insurance is not a model for preventative care. It's a much more complicated issue." –J. Manuel de la Rosa, M.D., Regional Dean, Texas Tech University Health Sciences Center at El Paso

Community Voices program leaders are enthusiastic about strides made through the initiative to date, but realistic about the work yet to be done. Programs established must be sustained. Pilot activities undertaken must be expanded. Lessons from one successful effort must be applied to work beginning in another venue. As part of this process, community health system stakeholders continue to push in one direction while political, economic, and marketplace dynamics are pulling the opposite way. The principles that govern their models – prevention, primary health care, and community outreach as essential elements; strong connections between public health, primary health care, health systems, and education; a broad definition of health that embraces physical, oral, and mental health services as well as employment, housing, education, transportation, and other social determinants of well-being – remain outside of the traditional medical model in most places. With health care and coverage costs rising and public resources strained by previous and current policy decisions,

Community Voices participants recognize that the time at hand is ever more precious.

Through the initiative, stakeholders in 13 communities have a few more years to learn from the strategies in place and share lessons with decision makers in health care and academic institutions, philanthropic organizations, and state and federal government. Community Voices program leaders say that this protected time is their greatest luxury – an interval for dialogue, creativity, and model development that they are working to solidify and sustain beyond the funding period. Time, according to most Community Voices program leaders, is a significant factor in their ability to build something better. Oftentimes in initiatives, communities are expected to show results in a year or two. So, as one project director says, "Community Voices is more than just funding. It is the overall investment of time and resources – investment that makes it possible to take risks and be successful."

By investing community will, Community Voices is building workable models.

But the other essential ingredients for success, Community Voices program leaders believe, are the resolve to pursue change and community readiness to collaborate. Community Voices models and products to date are indicative of the power of community will marshaled through collaboration. In the face of marketplace and fiscal pressures to cut back and do less, Community Voices participants have insisted on doing more to address real community needs by expanding access, reducing barriers, and streamlining processes to attract more underserved people into organized systems of care. They have found ways to do so by reorienting priorities, mining the resources at hand, and collaborating rather than competing. By investing community will, Community Voices is building workable models with the potential to inform policy and practice discussions.

Investment sparks action, participants say. And action yields additional investment. The Kellogg Foundation's investment in Community Voices – the funding, the six-year time frame, the conceptual framework for action, and the technical assistance – is helping communities to leverage more resources. The synergy of this level of investment – across the Community Voices network

161

and within individual communities – is the real value of the initiative, according to participants and observers alike. "Funders often 'dump money' into a problem," one participant says. "But there is a real value in putting resources behind the hub – the structure or process that brings people together."

Investments in the process are revealing more about health system vulnerabilities and opportunities as the work continues. As health departments seek to reorient practices to contribute to homeland security, the outreach and care management strategies that link health care systems with the most fragile communities take on added significance. As the limitations of health financing and delivery systems push more and more people to the margins, the growing cry for viable models of system change makes Community Voices collaborative products more instructive and useful. As employers and consumers express frustration with growing costs and the constraints of health systems in place, Community Voices participants' willingness to stand together and raise issues about access to care and coverage in the health care marketplace are broadening a national conversation about the need for fundamental health system change.

Community Voices participants know that health care is more than a market. They know, too, that the Community Voices model – its inclusive approach, principles, and priorities – has utility for other communities and insights that offer guidance to institutional and public policy decision makers. The Community Voices process illustrates some replicable ways to make sense of health care systems; its products underscore the potential. But perhaps more importantly, the level of engagement among health system stakeholders across traditional service, practice, and advocacy divides indicates that communities and providers have reached a promising state of readiness. They are poised and willing to be active partners in addressing community health issues and reorienting systems. And, when given the time and opportunity, they are more than eager to bring creativity and resolve to community collaborative efforts. Now, Community Voices program leaders believe, they are waiting to see who else is willing to "step up." To get things started, Community Voices participants say they willingly invite other funders, advocates, public agencies, health professions organizations, and government to join their efforts and commit to a collaborative process.

Acknowledgements

Community Voices: HealthCare for the Underserved reflects the dedication and insight of its grantees and their partners. But Community Voices also owes a great deal to the vision and guidance of a hardworking team of W.K. Kellogg Foundation program staff and administration whose enduring interest in expanding access to care and coverage for the most vulnerable led to the development and implementation of the initiative. Working closely with a Resource Team of advisors and consultants, these program leaders have been instrumental in supporting the work of Community Voices grantees.

Marguerite Johnson, *Vice President for Programs*
Gloria R. Smith, *Vice President for Programs, (retired January 2002)*
Henrie M. Treadwell, *Program Director*
C. Patrick Babcock, *Director of Public Policy*
Kay Randolph-Back, *Program Analyst*
Barbara Sabol, *Program Director*
Terri D. Wright, *Program Director*
Karen E. Lake, *Director of Marketing and Communications*
Jacquelynne Borden-Conyers, *Communications Manager*
Teresa Odden, *Program Assistant*
Celeste Etheridge, *Office Manager*
Kathy Reincke, *Communications Assistant*
Constance I. Vunovich, *Meeting Planner*

Hyde Park Communications, Washington, DC
Abt Associates, Inc., Cambridge, MA
Marguerite Ro, Columbia University, New York, NY

Writing: Mary B. Cohen, Kalamazoo, MI
Design: Designworks, Battle Creek, MI
Printing: United Book Press, Inc., Baltimore, MD

Resource Guide

Community Voices Learning Laboratories

Visit www.communityvoices.org

Alameda County/Oakland, California

Asian Health Services, Inc.
7700 Edgewater Drive
Suite 215
Oakland, CA 94621
(510) 633-6292
Fax (510) 567-1553

Albuquerque, New Mexico

University of New Mexico
Health Sciences Center
CRTC B-78
900 Camino de Salud Northeast
Albuquerque, NM 87131
(505) 272-4590
Fax (505) 272-3486

Baltimore, Maryland

Baltimore City Health Department
Division of Preventive Medicine and Epidemiology
3rd Floor
210 Guilford Avenue
Baltimore, MD 21202
(410) 396-4387
Fax (410) 396-1571

California Native Americans

California Rural Indian Health Board, Inc.
4400 Auburn Boulevard
2nd Floor
Sacramento, CA 95815
(916) 929-9761
Fax (916) 929-7246

Denver, Colorado

Denver Health & Hospital Authority
777 Bannock Street, MC 7779
Denver, CO 80204
(303) 436-4071
Fax (303) 436-4069

Detroit, Michigan

Voices of Detroit Initiative
4201 St. Antoine Boulevard
University Health Center-9C
Detroit, MI 48201
(313) 832-4246
Fax (313) 832-4308

El Paso, Texas

Community Voices, El Paso
1100 North Stanton, Suite 701
El Paso, TX 79902
(915) 545-4810
Fax (915) 545-2159

Lansing/Ingham County, Michigan

Ingham County Health Department
P.O. Box 30161
5303 South Cedar Street
Lansing, Michigan 48909
(517) 887-4311
Fax (517) 887-4310

Miami, Florida

Camillus House, Inc.
336 Northwest Fifth Street
Miami, FL 33128
(305) 374-1065 ext. 220
Fax (305) 372-1402

North Carolina

FirstHealth of the Carolinas, Inc.
P.O. Box 3000
155 Memorial Drive
Pinehurst, NC 28374
(910) 215-1922
Fax (910) 215-5054

Northern Manhattan, New York

Northern Manhattan Community Voices Collaborative
60 Haven Avenue, Suite 3B
New York, NY 10032
(212) 304-7032
Fax (212) 544-1905

Washington, DC

District of Columbia Department of Health
825 North Capitol Street, N.E.
Room 3109, Third Floor
Washington, DC 20002
(202) 442-9335
Fax (202) 535-1710

West Virginia

WV Higher Education Policy Commission
1018 Kanawha Boulevard East
Suite 1100
Charleston, WV 25301
(304) 558-0530
Fax (304) 558-0532